Smart Guide™
to
Buying
a
Home

About Smart Guides™

Welcome to Smart Guides. Each Smart Guide is created as a written conversation with a learned friend; a skilled and knowledgeable author guides you through the basics of the subject, selecting the most important points and skipping over anything that's not essential. Along the way, you'll also find smart inside tips and strategies that distinguish this from other books on the topic.

Within each chapter you'll find a number of recurring features to help you find your way through the information and put it to work for you. Here are the user-friendly elements you'll encounter and what they mean:

Buying a home is the largest single purchase most people make in their

The Keys
Each chapter opens by highlighting in overview style the most important concepts in the pages that follow.

Smart Money
Here's where you will learn opinions and recommendations from experts and professionals in the field.

Street Smarts
This feature presents smart ways in which people have dealt with related issues and shares their secrets for success.

Smart Sources
Each of these sidebars points the way to more and authoritative information on the topic, from organizations, corporations, and publications to Web sites and more.

Smart Definition
Terminology and key concepts essential to your mastering the subject matter are clearly explained in this feature.

F.Y.I.
Related facts, statistics, and quick points of interest are noted here.

The Bottom Line
The conclusion to each chapter, here is where the lessons learned in each section are summarized so you can revisit the most essential information of the text.

lifetimes, yet many people plunge into the process completely uninformed. The *Smart Guide to Buying a Home* is specifically designed to change that. It will literally make you "smarter" about everything involved in home buying, from how to shop for a mortgage to how to select a real estate agent or buyer's broker to how to minimize your closing costs—and it does so in a way that anyone can understand. Whether you're a first-timer or a current homeowner interested in trading up, the *Smart Guide to Buying a Home* will put you in control.

Smart Guide™

to

Buying
a
Home

Alfred and Emily Glossbrenner

CADER BOOKS

John Wiley & Sons, Inc.
New York • Chichester • Weinheim • Brisbane • Singapore • Toronto

Contents

Introduction

The problem with buying a home is that most people don't do it often enough to get really good at it. And make no mistake—it *is* a complicated process, with many steps and a lot of money on the line. On the other hand, ordinary men, women, and couples buy homes every day. And as you will discover, there is a cadre of professionals to guide you from beginning to end. The fact is, with the probable exception of your current landlord, just about everybody in society *wants* you to buy a home, and many institutions will do everything they can to help.

The message is: You can do this.

The mountain isn't nearly as tough to climb as it may now seem. But you want to do it the right way. You want to be smart about it. You don't need some book that treats you like a dummy or whose authors assume that every state in the Union does things the way they are done in California. Real estate transactions are quintessentially state-oriented functions, and differing state laws and local customs can have a big impact on you and your bank account.

You're No Dummy!

What you need is a book written by two professional explainers, one of whom just happens to have run the real estate licensing program for a major testing organization some years ago. You need a book written by people who are not associated with the real estate industry in any way. Look around: nearly every other book you'll find on the subject of home buying is written by someone who, for professional reasons, can't afford to offend anybody in the industry by telling it like it is.

For example, few other books emphasize the fact that "your" real estate agent does not work for you. No matter how friendly, charming, or interested in your family he or she may appear to be, "your" agent works for the seller. And, as you will learn later, should you tell this person the top price you would pay for a given house, he or she is *legally obligated* to pass that information on to the seller.

If you're like nearly 75 percent of home buyers, according to a Federal Trade Commission survey, that fact will come as a rather large surprise to you. Now that you know it, you're in a position to save thousands of dollars—just from reading only a few paragraphs of this book. You will find that the many paragraphs that follow contain equally valuable information, for this is a very consumer-oriented book. It will show you how the game is played and then teach you how to play it to maximum advantage.

Beginning with an Overview

Unlike nearly every other book on the subject, this one starts off with an overview of the home-buying process. The goal is to give you a conceptual framework so that as you work through this process, you'll not only know what happens next, you'll know where everything fits.

For example, did you know that once you are finally serious about buying a home, your first stop should be a local bank and not a local real estate agency? Chapter 1, "The Process of Buying a Home," explains why this is so. It also lets you know that most people do not need to make a down payment of 20 percent. Many borrowers can get a mortgage at a good interest rate by making a down payment of as little as 5 percent.

"Pros and Cons of Owning a Home," chapter 2, begins by doing everything it can to discourage you from buying a home. It opens with a "cold showers and root canal" discussion of the many downsides of home ownership. Frankly, buying a house, condo, town house, or co-op apartment is like having a kid. And there's really no point in fighting it:

• Step 1: Take out scissors and cut large hole in pocket.

• Step 2: Put money in pocket.

• Step 3: Repeat Step 2.

The chapter ends on the upside, however. For, be it ever so expensive, there truly is no place like home—for tax deductions, personal freedom, community, family, and any other "warm-and-fuzzies" you might care to add.

The next chapter, "How Much House Can You Afford?," is a toughie because it asks you to collect a lot of records and to do a lot of work figuring your net worth and getting your daily expenses down on paper. On the other hand, you're going to have to do this anyway when you apply for a mortgage, so why not do it sooner rather than later? The worksheets you will find here in chapter 3 will be a big help. Among other things, the chapter explains your FICO (First, Isaac Company) credit-rating score, something most other books on the subject overlook.

The progression is as logical as can be. Once you've decided that buying a home is what you want to do, and you've gotten a handle on how much you can afford, the next step is to think about where (and in what) you want to live. Chapter 4, "Homes and Locations," addresses this idea with the goal of opening your mind. As you will see, there really are homes everywhere. But there are many things to consider, location being only one of them.

Lots of Options

Chapter 5 is also designed to open your mind. It presents "Real Estate Agent Options," and, far from trashing real estate agents and brokers, praises them. But a traditional seller-paid real estate agent is no longer the only way one can go. In many areas, you can hire a "buyer's broker" or "buyer's agent" who will work for *you*, not for the seller. As you will see, *Money* magazine reports that people using such professionals generally save 5 percent or more when buying a home.

Chapter 6, "Evaluating Properties," is as hard-nosed as the rest of this book, if not more so. Your coauthors have lived in apartments (many of them) and know as well as anyone the thrill of imagining ourselves in a space we could call our own. The vision and desire tend to blind one to flaws in a property that would instantly raise red flags for a seasoned homeowner. There are no "perfect" homes, but this chapter will help you temper your enthusiasm and avoid making a serious mistake.

Chapter 7, "Offers and Negotiations," continues the drama by showing you what is likely to happen once you have identified a home you would like to buy. This is a crucial chapter for anyone who has never bought a home before. Whether you absolutely hate negotiating or revel in the give-and-take, Chapter 7 will give you the tools you need.

Finding the Money

There's just one problem. The process of buying a home chugs along on two tracks. Track 1 is the property, the owner, and the price. Track 2 is the matter of coming up with the money. That's what chapters 8 and 9 are all about. These chapters will show you what you need to know about mortgages and how to find the mortgage that's right for you. They alert you to the fact that there is an entire industry based on home-loan mortgages and that it has many "products" to offer. You really do have lots of options.

Equally important, you will learn that there are many federal and state programs aimed at making it easier to buy a home, and you do not have to be poverty-stricken to take advantage of them. In fact, even if you've owned many homes in your life, if you haven't owned one in the past two to three years, you are considered a "first-time buyer" for the purposes of many of these programs.

Chapter 10, the final chapter, appropriately enough, is "The Closing." The closing (or "making settlement" or "closing escrow") is the meeting at which everything is finalized—checks are written and legal documents are signed or initialed. This chapter will help you understand (and anticipate) closing costs. It will also alert you to such important steps as taking a final walk-through of the property just before the closing.

We Own It!

At this point, no one needs to list the benefits of home ownership or otherwise sell you on the idea of buying a home. If you're holding this book, you're already giving it serious consideration. What's likely to be most helpful is an image. It's the image of you (or you and your mate) an hour after you've signed the final papers.

You're standing in the living room of your new home. The moving van may be on the way, but just now the room is empty. And suddenly the reality hits. You look around and then at each other. "We did it!" you say. "We *own* this!"

You're about to embark on a great adventure. Like all adventures, it will have its ups and downs. But if you keep this image in mind, and keep this book close at hand, you'll be able to smoothly sail through the process to reach your goal—a home of your own.

The Process of Buying a Home

Fighter pilots are briefed on their coming missions in the "ready room." Wall Street attorneys receive similar "heads up" previews of the coming battle before a corporate takeover contest begins. Even high school football and Little League teams are prepped by their coaches before they take the field.

But no one gives the prospective home buyer the Big Picture. Because they know how everything works, bankers, lenders, appraisers, attorneys, and real estate agents often assume that you do as well—when in reality, that's usually not the case. And no one offers to put an arm over your shoulder, take you aside, and say, "Listen, here's how the process will unfold, and here's what you need to know about it going in."

That's what this book is designed to do in general, but it is what this chapter is intended to do in particular. Here is an overview, a rough cut, of the steps you will follow as you progress toward buying a home. Succeeding chapters provide much more detail and smooth many of the edges. But each one assumes that you have the entire process in mind as you read them. So read this chapter first.

First, Get Prequalified

After you've determined that you really are ready to buy a home, the first step is to look at your financial situation. If you've been steadily employed for the last two or three years and don't have too much debt (credit card, car loan, student loan, or others), you can almost certainly qualify for a mortgage of some sort. The worksheets in chapter 3 will help you get a handle on your finances in an organized fashion.

Next, consider getting prequalified by a lender. Make an appointment with the mortgage-lending officer at your local bank. Bring in your worksheets and ask the individual to help you figure out how large a mortgage you qualify for. And ask if he or she would be willing to issue a letter stating his or her findings.

There is no cost or obligation to getting prequalified. The lender will happily take a look at your numbers in hopes of getting your business. Prequalifying serves as a reality check. Eventually, you will want to get preapproved for a given loan amount, and that does involve one or more fees. But that's in the future.

You now have an idea of the maximum you can borrow and what your monthly mortgage payment will be. But you may not want to take such a large loan. Be realistic about the impact that owning a home will have on your lifestyle. And realize that there are many home-buying costs you may not be aware of if you've never done it before.

Down Payment and Closing Costs

You will need to make a down payment of 5 to 20 percent in most cases. And some portion of that amount will be due weeks before you get a check from the lender to actually buy your house. That's because the seller will want you to make a deposit when you both sign the Real Estate Purchase Contract (REPC). The need to come up with thou-

F.Y.I.

Private mortgage insurance (PMI) will be required if you make a down payment of less than 20 percent. You will be charged anywhere from 0.22 to 0.9 percent of the loan amount as a PMI premium for insurance that protects the lender should you default on the loan. However, once your equity reaches 20 percent, either because of the payments you have made or an increase in the market value of your home, PMI is no longer necessary. Beginning in 1999, lenders will be required to automatically cancel PMI insurance once their records indicate that your equity has risen to 22 percent, but don't wait for the lender. Actively monitor the situation yourself.

sands of dollars so soon takes many buyers by surprise. So plan for it.

If your down payment is less than 20 percent, the lender will insist that you buy private mortgage insurance (PMI). The lender will want to know where your down payment is coming from. And while you might think that using money given to you by parents or relatives is a simple answer, lenders often view such gifts as loans that increase your indebtedness. You may be required to supply a "gift letter" in which the relative says that the money is indeed a gift, not a loan.

On the other hand, you may be able to borrow the needed funds from your retirement plan or plans. This may or may not be a good idea. But anyone with a Roth IRA can borrow a lifetime limit of $10,000 from it for the purpose of buying or building a house for him- or herself or for a spouse, child, grandchild, or parent who is a "first-time buyer." Whether you can borrow from your 401(k) or not depends on how the rules of your company's plan are written.

You also need to think about closing costs. Your lender will probably charge you a certain number of points for making the loan, payable when you close the deal and sign the final papers. Each point is equal to 1 percent of the loan amount. Points can often be folded into the mortgage. This increases your indebtedness, but it eliminates the need to come up with the cash.

The other costs associated with the closing usually cannot be sidestepped so easily. You will need money to pay for homeowner's insurance, title insurance, and possibly flood insurance. You'll have to pay a pro-rated share of the real estate and school taxes associated with the property. There may be charges for termite and other inspections, for a land survey, and for transfer taxes levied by local governments. In all, closing costs, including lender's points, will add up to between 3 and 6 percent of the loan amount, or 2 to 5 percent of the purchase price.

And after all this—after you shake hands with everyone once the papers are all signed—you still have to move your stuff into your new dwelling and possibly pay for interior painting and other spruce-up and "moving-in" expenses.

So Much, So Soon

Digging so deeply into the financial side of things so early in the process may seem overly analytical, but there are good reasons for doing so. First, before anyone can go looking at a property, they have to develop some idea of what they can afford.

Second, there is no point in simply muddling through when the facts are all clearly visible. If you buy *this* house, you will have *these* expenses. Certainly some costs are not predictable. But if you pay attention as you read this book, there shouldn't be any major expense surprises.

Third, when you fall in love with a house, you will rationalize. You will tell yourself that you can cut back here or there in order to make the payments. You will convince yourself that you can do the necessary repair work yourself, even though you've never held a power tool in your life. You may still buy the house, but by concentrating on the financials first, you will know exactly what you're getting into.

Finally, most real estate agents will want you to fill out a form presenting your financial information so they can get an idea of how much house you can afford. You do not have to do this. And you may not

SMART DEFINITION

First-time buyer

Government laws and mortgage programs do not define this term as you'd expect. For most, a first-time buyer is someone who has not owned a home in the previous two years. So even if you've owned several homes in the past, if you've been renting for the past two years, you are a first-time buyer as far as the government is concerned.

F.Y.I.

Because they work for the seller, real estate agents will do everything they can to get you to pay the highest possible price. Fortunately, in many areas you'll have the option of hiring a "buyer's agent." This may be a conventional real estate agent who has agreed in writing to represent you for a fee, or it may be someone who represents buyers exclusively. As you will learn later, going the buyer's agent route can save you as much as 5 percent on the transaction.

want to. The agent may be a personal friend or acquaintance to whom you'd rather not reveal such information. More important, as you will hear repeatedly throughout this book, "your" real estate agent doesn't work for you. He or she works for the seller and, as mentioned earlier, is required by law to pass on any information you supply.

Clearly, the less "your" agent knows about your finances, the better. Still, you can't blame an agent for wanting to avoid wasting time with someone who is not financially able to buy. That's why it can be a good idea to give the agent a copy of your pre-qualification letter from a bank or other lender.

Selecting an Agent

Once you've taken a clear-eyed look at your financial situation, you may or may not decide that you're ready to buy. The loan officer may suggest that you pay off more of your debt or replace your expensive new car with a reliable used one. Or you may decide that you're just not ready to settle down.

Whatever you do, make sure you aren't buying for the wrong reasons. If your apartment lease is about to expire and you don't want to renew, consider moving in with family or friends to give yourself the extra time you need to really shop for a house. With all the self-storage facilities available these days, it's not too tough to find a place to store your belongings for several months. Or consider the penalties of breaking your lease six months from now. Are they really all that significant?

Do not let yourself be rushed. And, even more important, do not let yourself be influenced by some self-imposed deadline. In a word, *relax.* Easy to say once you've been around the course several times, not so easy to do if this is your first time out. But try. Pull back and take the time to think.

This is particularly important when selecting a real estate agent. Do not blindly go with one of your parents' friends or even one of your own friends. A really good agent can make a big difference, and too much money is involved to be worried about hurting someone's feelings. So ask around. You're going to be paying whomever you choose thousands of dollars, whether as part of the seller's price or as a fee. It just makes sense to get some recommendations, if possible.

Location and Type

When you begin to get really serious about buying a home, you need to think about location. Do not assume you have to live in one particular area. Put a pin anywhere on a map, and within a fifty-mile radius of that point there will be many neighborhoods and "locations," some of which will be much more desirable than others. Why? School districts, for one thing. Taxes, proximity to commuting routes and mass transit facilities, quality and price of homes, sense of community among residents, and many other characteristics set apart the "best" locations.

Be similarly open-minded about what constitutes a "home." Town houses, condos, big-city co-op apartments, and detached single-family homes are all part of the mix. Remember that whatever you buy now won't necessarily be your "ultimate home." But as long as it is a quality property in a desirable location, you can't go wrong. That's

"My husband is a bit of a mouse," reports Roberta, 32, the checkout-line supervisor at a large grocery store. "We'd probably seen a dozen houses and were seriously considering two of them. Then we drove by one with a new For Sale sign. John was embarrassed to ask our agent to set up a showing. 'She's spent a lot of time on us already,' he said.

"I told him to do the math. On a $150,000 house, she'll make at least $2,250. At $20 an hour, she'd have to work fourteen full days for us and only us to earn that much. That's like three five-day weeks. There's no way she's put in that kind of time for us. So *I* called, and guess what? That's the house we bought. My advice is don't be shy. If real estate agents weren't so well paid, there wouldn't be so many of them."

because once you buy, you will start to build equity instead of throwing your money away on rent each month. And, even in the worst case, you can almost always sell a property for at least what you paid for it.

Negotiations

There *are* no perfect properties. But regardless of your price range, there are many that you will find not only acceptable but downright desirable. You've got a handle on your finances, so you know what you can afford and what you can borrow. You've identified several locations and looked at properties in each of them. Now you've found one property in particular that you like. One that you *really* like.

Don't say a word to the real estate agent, unless you're using a buyer's agent or buyer's broker. Be cool. Allow as how you might see yourself living here, "But what do you think, honey?" Your honey shrugs, just like you rehearsed it. "Well, I don't know. We'd have to gut the kitchen, and look at this wallpaper—ugh!" Anything you say will be reported to the seller. So don't express any more than "mild interest," even if the two of you are silently saying, "Yes, yes, a thousand times yes. This is the house we want!"

The next day, you phone your agent and say that you might like to make an offer. That will get the agent's attention in a New York second. But you know what? First you'd like to see the "comps." You'd like to have the agent put together a list of comparable properties that have sold in the last six months.

This shouldn't take too long, but it is an important step. At the very least it protects you from overpaying when you're moving from a different area of the country and might not have a good sense of this new area's prices. And regardless of where you are moving from, it taps you into the market and shows you what properties are selling for there.

Shopping for a Lender

One step you can take to make your negotiating position even stronger is to get preapproved by a lender. So as you're shopping for a house, start shopping for a lender. Chapters 8 and 9 will be a big help. As you will discover, there are many kinds of loans and many special programs. You may be able to get a mortgage by putting as little as 3 to 5 percent down, not the 20 percent that for years was the customary down payment.

And everything is negotiable. So you can play one lender against another. Money is ultimately just a product, and lenders make no profit if they can't persuade you to "buy" that product from them.

Once you've selected a lender, you'll have to pay a loan application fee of about $225 and supply much more financial information than when you were being prequalified. If you're self-employed or otherwise have an erratic cash flow, you may be able to get a *no-doc* or *low-doc* (short for *documentation*) loan that requires far fewer financial details in return for a slightly higher interest rate.

The lender will then issue a commitment letter promising to loan you a certain amount of money, provided the property you eventually select is

SMART MONEY

According to Leo J. Berard, charter president of the National Association of Exclusive Buyer Agents, first-time buyers today are better educated than ever before. "But we have to slow down the process, making sure people realize the pros and cons of a property before they buy."

Also, while it is tempting to act quickly to get a particular interest rate, according to Berard, seasoned buyers know that even if they have to accept a mortgage with a higher-than-average rate, it is the careful selection of the home itself that's more important in the long run. That's because you can always refinance when rates fall in the future.

SMART MONEY

The Mortgage Almanac (mortgagealmanac.com) interviewed John Schleck, regional manager with PNC Mortgage, about interest rate lock-ins. Should you lock-in or float? "If a floating rate is going to keep you up at night between application and closing, you should consider locking in. Keep in mind, for most people, what we are talking about is a savings of ten to twenty dollars per month if interest rates change by an eighth of a percent or a quarter of a percent. . . . In fact, a number of lenders today offer a 'float-down' option, which gives consumers the ability to take advantage of improvements in rates prior to closing."

The Almanac further advises to get all rate locks in writing and to make sure the lock-in is from the actual lender if you are using a mortgage broker.

appraised at a sufficiently high value. You should also ask the lender for a written "lock-in" or "rate-lock" commitment. This is the lender's promise to offer you the money at the same terms that exist today (interest rate, points, length of term). Lock-ins typically expire in thirty to sixty days.

Making the Deal

Your negotiations, mediated by your real estate agent, are likely to go back and forth. You want the KitchenAid dishwasher; they want to take it with them. So you say, "Fine, take it, but we'd like you to leave the drapes in the dining room." Or you offer to pay the sellers the current fair market value for the dishwasher.

Negotiating to purchase a home should not be a scorched-earth, take-no-prisoners process. And even though emotions can run high on both sides, a good real estate agent will keep the deal moving and never let things get out of hand.

Contingencies

Real estate transactions always involve conditions, or *contingencies*. You say, in effect, "We will pay you X dollars for your property, provided that . . ." One of the most important contingencies for both parties is the buyers' commitment to pay the down payment and the agreed balance, provided they can get a loan for that amount at a certain interest rate and term.

That's right: when you buy a home, the terms of your loan are part of the purchase contract. If you can't get that loan, the deal falls through. This is the last thing the sellers want. Not only does it mean that they have to start all over with someone else, it means that the property has been off the market and thus unavailable to another buyer while they were dealing with you.

That's why being preapproved for your loan is such a powerful negotiating tool. In return for the certainty that there will be no problem with your loan, a seller may be willing to accept a somewhat lower price or pay other costs.

Another important contingency is the engineering report. All smart buyers make their sales contracts and offers contingent on having the property inspected by a licensed home inspector (someone who is usually an engineer). Should the inspector discover any problems, these factors will become items for negotiation.

Sealing the Deal

When you make your initial offer, you will have to accompany it with a *binder,* or *earnest money*—typically a few hundred to one thousand dollars. Once the deal has been hammered out and the contract has been signed, you will probably have to make a deposit of several thousand dollars. All of this money counts toward your down payment. The deposit money will be placed in an interest-bearing account in most cases. In fact, this should be one of the terms of the contract.

Another item in the contract will be the date of your closing. That's the day you meet with the seller to "make settlement," as they say in some parts of the country. Californians and other westerners call it "escrow," while people in other states call it "the closing."

Ideally, one of the contingencies in your purchase contract will be a final walk-through just prior to closing. This gives you the chance to make sure that there have been no changes in the house since you agreed to buy it and that the sellers have indeed left the dishwasher and fulfilled other conditions of the agreement.

Procedures and customs vary with each state and locality, but wherever you are, someone will be in charge of making sure that all the documents are signed or initialed in the correct places and that all the funds end up in the proper hands. When it's over, you will quite literally be handed the keys and be ready to begin life in your new home.

The Grand Adventure

This is the main outline of the home-buying process. Details will vary with the state and with local custom. But in almost every case, the process involves these steps, pretty much in this order. There is a lot more you need to know. But as you read the following chapters, you will find it very helpful to keep this overview in mind.

You'll also find it helpful to remember that the only way you can really lose in real estate is by not buying *something*. To put it another way, imagine a Supreme Being saying, "You're going to have to pay $800 a month to have a roof over your head. This is not negotiable. But you have the choice of burning eight crisp $100 bills each month or depositing them in a savings account. What is your decision?"

The other thing you need to be aware of is the

incredible number of sources of financing and special programs that exist. (See chapter 9 for an exhaustive list.) Truly, if you can rent, you can own, and there are many ways to overcome the down-payment and closing-costs hurdles.

So let's get started. It is your coauthors' fondest hope that reading this book will change your life. We've "been there, done that," and we will take good care of you.

THE BOTTOM LINE

Buying a home is a "life event." It's not something you do every day. It involves a lot of money and a lot of unfamiliar terms, steps, and procedures. But you have at least two things very much in your favor.

First, the sellers who own the property you eventually decide to buy probably don't have much more experience than you do. And second, if you pay attention to the market for both homes and mortgage loans, you're unlikely to overpay, and if you do, it won't be by much.

Finally, remember that everything in a real estate deal, with the exception of government-imposed transfer and other taxes, is negotiable. All you need is knowledge, and that's what you'll find in this book.

....

Pros and Cons of Owning a Home

As Monty Python fans know, one of the classic comedy lines of all time is "No one expects the Spanish Inquisition!" Whether you're a Python fan or not, however, you probably don't expect a chapter in a book of this sort specifically designed to *discourage* you from buying a home. But here it is, and it is no laughing matter.

The Downside of Home Ownership

Actually, only the first half of the chapter is devoted to the downside of home ownership. The second half presents the positive aspects. So you might think of it as a Marine Corps boot camp program designed to first break you down and then to rebuild you in the image of the Corps. Except that there is no image and no Corps. What there is, among many home buyers, is a less than full appreciation of just what they're getting into.

Treat this chapter as a reality check. Forget the warm-and-fuzzies. Owning your own home is immensely satisfying on many different levels, and it is the smart thing to do financially for all kinds of reasons. But it is also a huge responsibility, something most people tend to forget once the home-buying bug bites.

The Financial Risks

Buying a house exposes you to several serious financial hazards. For example, should you default on your mortgage, you could lose your entire down payment. That can be as much as 5 to 20 percent of the price of the house. Should you be unable to make your mortgage payments, the lender can foreclose on the property and sell it to pay off the loan.

Lenders do not like to do this. Most will work with you to restructure your loan so that your monthly payment is lower. Many will offer credit counseling to help you get your credit-card debt and other finances under control. But if they must foreclose, lenders are under no obligation to sell the property for its full market value and refund your down payment. Their main concern is selling the house for a price high enough to cover the outstanding balance of the mortgage.

There are other financial risks as well. Should someone taking a shortcut across your backyard slip on wet grass and break his arm, you can be sued—even though you never gave permission for him to be on your property. A tree falling on your house could completely destroy your kitchen. The pipes in the unheated downstairs powder room could freeze and burst while you're on a winter ski vacation. Or maybe it'll be the high-pressure hoses hooked up to your washing machine that spring a leak while you're away.

Of course, this is why you buy insurance. But you can't insure against everything, and even if you could, the monthly premiums would be out of sight. Practically speaking, when something happens to your house, it's going to cost you time and money, no matter how much insurance you have.

SMART SOURCES

The federal government offers scores of low- or no-cost publications to help with the home-buying process, including *How to Buy a Home with a Low Down Payment* (566E, free), *The HUD Homebuying Guide* (567E, free), and *Buying Your Home: Settlement Costs and Helpful Information* (112E, $1.75). If you have Internet access, you can view and print any publication free of charge. Or you can write or call for a free catalog.

Consumer Information
  Center
Pueblo, CO 81009
719-948-4000
(Monday–Friday,
  9 A.M.–4:30 P.M. EST)
www.pueblo.gsa.gov

Maintenance: Time and Money

Having a lawn and garden—your own bit of earth—holds great appeal for many prospective home buyers. But even if you're not fanatical about weeds, just a small lawn can be a lot of work. At the very least, you'll have to mow regularly. So where will the time come from? Which of your current nonwork activities will you have to cut short or give up each week? Or do you plan to pay someone to do the lawn for you, and if so, how much?

In many areas of the country, when the lawn mowing ends, the leaf raking begins, followed by the snow shoveling. And unlike the other two, shoveling the snow from a sidewalk in front of your house may be a legal obligation. Fail to do it, and you can be fined.

Outside chores like these are only the beginning. That rambling white colonial you've fallen in love with may lose some of its charm once you realize that you'll have to spend as much as $10,000 each time you have it painted, and that it will need painting every five to seven years. You can avoid that expense by choosing a brick or vinyl-clad house, although you may still have to have the windows and trim work painted regularly.

Speaking of windows, who will be washing yours? If the house doesn't have "triple-track" windows, someone will have to install the screens in the summer and storm windows once the weather turns cold. Of course, when temperatures drop, you'll be cozy in front of the fireplace—which may temporarily be your only source of heat while you're waiting for the service technician to come awaken your furnace from its summer slumber. And did you remember to have the chimney swept? More than one house has burned down due to a chimney fire fueled by accumulated pine tar and creosote.

These are just a few of the nonoptional chores of home ownership. There are many more. Most are not hugely time-consuming or terribly expensive should you decide to pay someone else to do them. But the time and the money required mounts up: fifty dollars here, a couple hundred there, a Saturday morning, a Sunday afternoon, evening hours after work. Worse still, not only do chores like these never end, they merely maintain your quality of life. They don't add value or get you ahead the way, say, redecorating a room, remodeling a kitchen, or buying a new appliance might.

Just Staying Even

It's actually even worse than that. A 1998 study commissioned by the *Wall Street Journal* concludes that "almost every house, no matter how recently or expertly built, is a money pit." The study found that keeping a typical home up to current standards for thirty years can cost almost four times the purchase price. Indeed, according to some experts, it may actually be cheaper to buy a new or fully remodeled home every ten years than to deal with the mounting repair problems that occur as your current home ages.

The biggest repair problems tend to occur when a home is between ten and twenty years old. "Many items start to fail then," says Gopal Ahluwalia, research director at the National Association of Home Builders. Buying a brand-new

SMART SOURCES

The Fannie Mae Foundation offers a free home-buying guide in English, Chinese, Vietnamese, Portuguese, Russian, Korean, Spanish, Haitian-Creole, and Polish. You may order online or by phone.

Fannie Mae Foundation
800-611-9566
www.homebuyingguide.
 org

Fannie Mae's HomePath site on the World Wide Web offers information, resources, checklists, and short quizzes designed to help you every step of the way.

Fannie Mae HomePath
800-732-6643
www.homepath.com

house can help, but only for a few years. According to the National Association of Home Builders, the average yearly maintenance and repair costs for a house built in 1990 is only about one third less than for one built before 1960.

To put some dollar figures on the table, here is what housing economist Robert Sheehan, who conducted the study for the *Wall Street Journal*, calculated for major repair and replacement costs on an upscale hypothetical brick house over thirty years. Keep in mind that even if you can do without such improvements yourself, you may have to make them anyway to be sure of getting the best price for your house when you sell.

Bathroom update	$26,194
Kitchen update (minor)	7,743
Kitchen update (major)	29,767
Exterior paint (trim only, three times)	911
Interior paint (four times)	9,161
Carpet replacement (three times)	10,201
Furnace/Air conditioning	3,088
Water heater	642
Roofing	2,082
Insulation	68
Window replacement	9,796
Door replacement and garage-door openers	1,861
Deck addition and replacement	18,905
New light fixtures	191
Six ceiling fans	1,323
Smoke detector	105
Washer replacement	466
Dryer replacement	348
Finish basement and one update	17,934

Taxes: More Bad News

Remember the Revolutionary War battle cry "No taxation without representation?" You may not know it, but in many areas of the country your property taxes can be increased by hundreds of dollars a year without your approval. Should you refuse to pay, the locality that imposed the levy can eventually seize your house and offer it at a sheriff's auction to anyone willing to pay your back taxes.

Or someone might move in next door who likes to play loud music while hosing down his boat in the drive—every Sunday at 6:00 A.M. Apartment dwellers are subject to similar nuisance neighbors, but they can ask the owner or building superintendent to intervene. Or they can enlist the help of fellow renters. But when you own a home and your next-door neighbors elect to park an ugly thirty-foot blue motor home in their driveway for nine months of the year, there's not much you can do.

Neighbors have pets. They have kids. They have parties. All of which can have a negative impact on you, and none of which you can do much about. Then you learn that some millionaire builder of "executive homes" wants to turn a nearby cornfield into a town house community that will boost traffic and congestion and at the very least require a tax increase to pay for more teachers, more schools, and improved roads and sewers.

You can try to fight it—democratic principles still apply—but it will cost you time and money, and you will probably lose in the end because, despite what they may say, everyone from local politicians to local shopkeepers benefits from development.

F.Y.I.

When you consider mortgage points, application and appraisal fees, home inspection expenses, title insurance, moving expenses, real estate agent commissions, and the other costs of buying or selling a home, a property has to appreciate nearly 15 percent for you to just break even when you sell it.

Home Ownership Costs: A Wake-Up Call

Here's a list of the time and/or money costs you can expect to encounter once you own a home, condominium, or apartment. Not all items apply to everyone, and certainly not all will occur in a given year. But this list of completely common and ordinary expenses should start you thinking about the true costs of home ownership.

Basic Ownership Costs

• Mortgage payments (principal and interest)

• Private mortgage insurance (PMI)

• Real estate taxes

• Homeowner's insurance

• Homeowner association dues and assessments

• Electricity

• Gas

• Water and sewer services

• Septic system maintenance (if you don't have sewers)

• Trash pickup

• Monthly alarm company fees

• Extermination services (mice, bugs, spiders, etc.)

Physical Plant Maintenance

• Furnace or heater service contract

• Furnace filters (forced-air systems)

• Air conditioner unit maintenance (whole-house)

• Clearing drain lines of tree roots

• Changing water filters

The Plus Side

So much for the downside. Owning a home is always more expensive than you think it will be, even if you buy a brand-new development home or condo. But if you buy a quality property in a good location, the benefits of home ownership, both psychic and financial, almost always out-

- Salt for water softener

- Pump replacement (if you use well water)

- Carpentry to repair or replace rotted wood

Exterior Maintenance

- Professional landscaping (optional)

- Weeding and flower bed maintenance

- Tree service to remove or trim trees

- Tree spraying for a variety of pests

- Lawn cutting

- Leaf raking

- Snow removal

- Gutter cleaning

- Window cleaning

- Roof replacement

- Repointing masonry

- Resurfacing or sealing driveway

- House painting

- Power washing to remove mildew from siding

Interior Maintenance

- Carpet and rug replacement

- Interior painting

- Hardwood floor cleaning, waxing, and buffing

- Recaulking and regrouting loose bathroom tiles

- Repairing or replacing major kitchen appliances

- Routine plumbing and electrical repairs

- Chimney sweeping

weigh the negatives. That's because, come what may, the vast majority of people in this country want to own their own homes.

Every human being understands this. The desire to stake out a patch of land and declare "This is mine!" is built into our very natures. Therefore, if you take the steps necessary to acquire a property, you will never have to worry about being able to sell it. There will always be a

SMART MONEY

Bill FitzPatrick of the American Success Institute says, "Let's suppose the tax benefits of home ownership were completely eliminated. Would your home still be the best investment you could ever hope to make?"

Assuming an annual appreciation of 6 percent and a house worth $100,000, in the first year the value of the home would increase by $6,000. But your yield is far greater. Why? "Because of leverage. You need only a modest down payment to control the asset. If you put $20,000 down, your yield is 30 percent. If you put only $5,000 down, your yield is 120 percent. And that's just in the first year. Even if all the other benefits of buying were eliminated, the combination of appreciation and leverage make home ownership an outstanding investment package."

demand. You may not always be able to get the price you want for it, but in most areas of the country, the value of your home will increase at least as fast as inflation.

Financial and Tax Benefits

There's an old saying among real estate professionals, "Renting is the same as owning. Except you're paying someone *else's* mortgage." In point of fact, you're paying even more than that. Every smart landlord builds maintenance, management, and tax costs into the rent that he or she charges. And few would put up with the hassles of being a landlord if they didn't also add a percentage for profit.

So look around your apartment. Whatever its square footage, if you're currently paying the market rate, you can almost certainly be paying the same amount per month to *own*, maintain, and pay the taxes on the same amount of space. The space may not be in the location you'd most prefer, but it will be yours, and you will no longer be kissing your money good-bye each month as you mail off your rent check.

Instead, you'll be building *equity*. You will own something whose value will increase over time. Several years from now, you will probably be able to sell this asset at a profit should you want to do so. And in the meantime, as its market value rises, your equity will increase. Before long, you will be in a position to borrow against your equity at very favorable interest rates because the loan will be secured by your property. You may not want a home-equity loan, but it is awfully nice to have that option.

And all this is before Uncle Sam lends his helping hand. As you will see throughout this book, increased home ownership is in everyone's interest, and many institutions do their best to make owning a home as affordable as possible. Certainly the biggest boost in this area comes from the federal government, which allows you to reduce your taxable income by whatever you pay in mortgage interest and real estate taxes.

What's the deduction worth in dollars and cents? To find out, multiply your monthly mortgage payment by your tax bracket. Because of the way lenders do things, during the first years of a mortgage, almost all of what you pay is applied toward interest. So if you're in the 28 percent tax bracket and pay $500 a month, the mortgage interest deduction is worth $140 a month. To put it another way, because it is tax deductible, that $500 actually costs you 28 percent less, or $360.

Tax Brackets
(based on 1998 tax rates)

Taxable Income	Tax Bracket
Single Taxpayer	
Under $25,350	15%
$25,350 to $61,400	28%
$61,400 to $128,100	31%
$128,100 to $278,450	36%
Over $278,450	39.6%

(continued)

Taxable Income	Tax Bracket
Married Couple Filing Jointly	
Under $42,350	15%
$42,350 to $102,300	28%
$102,300 to 155,950	31%
$155,950 to $278,450	36%
Over $278,450	39.6%

If You Can Rent, You Can Own

It is impossible to overemphasize the financial benefits of owning over renting. When projecting into the future, the fact that your rent will increase over time ranks right up there with the certainty of death and taxes. So whatever you're paying today, you can bet you'll be paying more in the future.

There's another old saying in real estate, "If you can afford to rent, you can afford to own." Take it on faith that if you are currently paying $500 a month in rent, you can pay out the same amount monthly toward buying a $100,000 home.

You may think that this blithely ignores the challenge of saving enough money for the down payment and other costs of buying a home. But you're probably not aware that you can buy a home with as little as 3 to 5 percent down.

For example, on a $100,000 house, 3 percent down amounts to $3,000. Assume that closing costs add another $2,000. That means you can buy a $100,000 house with cash totaling only $5,000. Your mortgage loan will be $97,000. If you get a 30-year fixed-rate loan at 6.75 percent, your monthly mortgage payment will be $636. But, as you now know, if you are in the 28 percent tax bracket, that $636 actually costs you about $458.

This scenario is based on the Fannie 97 program underwritten by Fannie Mae, a government-chartered organization you'll learn more about later. The monthly figure does not include property taxes, private mortgage insurance, or homeowner's insurance costs. But then, you don't have to buy a $100,000 home either. In some areas of the country you can get a nice house for considerably less. And Fannie 97 is only one of many low-down-payment programs.

The point of this example is to start you thinking. It offers some real numbers to underscore the idea that if you can rent, you can own. Indeed, as you will see later, if you have decent credit and a good employment history, institutions and lenders will bend over backward to help you buy your first home.

F.Y.I.

According to the Office of Federal Housing Enterprise Oversight, the national average home appreciation for the sixty months (five years) between 1992 and 1997 was 17.1 percent. Utah led the country with an average 74.4 percent increase in resale values for the period. The national home appreciation rate for 1997 was 4.5 percent.

Warm-and-Fuzzies

With all of the hard, practical "heavy lifting" out of the way, you can give yourself permission to feel the warm-and-fuzzies of prospective home ownership. Considering the amount of money involved, it only makes good sense to buy a house with your head and not with your heart. But there's no denying the emotional component.

Just be aware that if you've spent the last couple of years in a cramped apartment, you are especially vulnerable to the emotional appeal of more space and the freedom to plant, paint, and redecorate as you please. Real estate agents know this.

Like all salespeople, they will pick up on your positive reactions and nurture them.

Buying a home, particularly a first home, should be a joyous experience. But it will be more satisfying still if you go in with your eyes open, aware of the risks and expenses involved. If you're still not discouraged after all that you've learned here, turn to the next chapter to discover just how much house you can afford!

THE BOTTOM LINE

Buying a home involves serious financial risks. It also involves considerable expenditures of time and money that most first-time buyers rarely consider. Insurance, taxes, never-ending maintenance, and assorted fees can eat up all your spare cash each month as well as all your spare time. And unlike a renter, you can't just pick up and go someplace else.

On the other hand, the financial and tax benefits of home ownership are so great that anyone who's ready to settle down should seriously consider buying instead of renting. In the majority of cases, if you can rent, you can own, sometimes with a down payment as small as 3 to 5 percent.

How Much House Can You Afford?

Avoiding the "Too Much House" Trap

Most home buyers, particularly first-timers, worry about whether the bank will be willing to lend them enough money to buy the home they want. Few worry about a bank lending them *more* than they can afford to repay. Yet this can be a serious problem. Like salespeople everywhere, loan officers and real estate agents aren't in the business of discouraging you from buying. They are in the business of getting you to spend as much of your income with them as possible.

Nice people though they may be, they do not care that your monthly payments may leave no extra money for furniture, vacations, or investments. As long as you meet their specifications, lenders will usually agree to loan you the maximum amount you can qualify for based on your total income, all outstanding debt, and down-payment requirements.

But taking them up on the offer to borrow "the max" can be a mistake. It isn't just the crimp the payments may put in your lifestyle. It's a matter of stretching yourself so thin that there's no margin for the unexpected. What if disaster strikes? What if you lose your job or become disabled? What if you or your partner develops a serious illness? With no financial wiggle room, you might be forced to sell your house at a loss. In extreme cases, the lender might be forced to foreclose, seize your house, and sell it to pay back the loan. In that case, you'd lose not only the house but your down payment and any equity you'd built up as well.

Keep Those Pencils Sharp!

This is not meant to scare you. It is just a gentle reminder to keep your pencils sharp, and to point out that the mortgage you can qualify for and the mortgage you can comfortably afford may be two very different things.

That said, you should know that if you've got good credit and a solid work record, the odds are very much in your favor. You may not be able to buy your dream house the first time out. But government agencies and private institutions alike are strongly motivated to do everything they can to get you into a house. In fact, as you will learn in a later chapter, in 1994 the federal government announced a National Home Ownership Strategy designed to boost home ownership from the 1994 level of 64 percent to 67.5 percent by the year 2000.

Many special programs are available. The place most people should start is with what the bank is willing to lend. And that usually is based on certain key ratios. (For simplicity, the word *bank* is used in this chapter and throughout this book to refer to any kind of lender. As you'll learn later, actual banks are but one of many different mortgage sources.)

Ratios, Ratios, and More Ratios

Here's the way we'd all like it to be: The kindly small-town banker puts his hand on your shoulder and says, "I've known your family—all of them—for over forty years. I will be happy to make this

One "quick-and-dirty" way to estimate how much house you can afford is to apply the "2½ Rule." Simply multiply your household's gross (pre-tax) income by 2 or 2½ to get a rough idea of what you can afford. Note, however, that this formula assumes interest rates of about 10 percent, a 20 percent down payment, excellent credit, and no debt.

loan so that you two can buy your first home." It was probably never really like this, but there can be no doubt that mortgage lending today is far less personalized than it was in the past. To a large extent, that's because home mortgages have become investment commodities.

In the past, banks, savings and loans, and other lenders would keep your mortgage in their loan portfolios. The interest and principal you paid would go straight to them and be loaned out in other mortgages. Today, most mortgage loans are bundled into packages of securities and sold to financial institutions that then sell shares in them to investors. This is called the *secondary* mortgage market, and it is the primary reason most loans have to be pretty much alike in terms of quality and risk.

Which is to say, they must meet the same standards. That's where the ratios come in. Fannie Mae Corporation (formerly the Federal National Mortgage Association) is the largest buyer in this market, so if it says it wants borrowers to have a debt-to-income ratio of no more than a certain percent, you can bet that mortgage lenders pay attention.

You'll learn more about Fannie Mae, Freddie Mac, and similar institutions later in this book. Right now it's important to be aware that each year (usually in December), Fannie Mae announces the largest-size mortgage it will buy. If your mortgage exceeds the Fannie Mae limit, you cannot get Fannie Mae–based financing. For 1998, the Fannie Mae limit for single-family houses was $227,150 in all parts of the country except Alaska, Hawaii, and the Virgin Islands, where it's $340,725.

The 28/36 Qualifying Ratios

The quick handle on the two most important Fannie Mae ratios is this:

• **The housing expense ratio.** Your total monthly housing costs should not exceed 28 percent of your monthly gross (pre-tax) income. The total housing cost figure is often called PITI, which stands for "principal, interest, taxes, and insurance," though it goes without saying that condominium or co-op fees are included as well, if applicable.

• **The total debt-to-income ratio.** Your total debt payments for the month—meaning your monthly housing costs plus payments for car loans, student loans, credit-card debt, and so forth—should not be more than 36 percent of your monthly gross income.

These ratios generally assume that you'll be making a down payment of 10 percent or more. But as Fannie Mae's own HomePath Web site (www.homepath.com) notes, "These lender ratios are flexible guidelines. If you have a consistent record of paying rent that is very close in amount to your proposed monthly mortgage payments, or if you make a large down payment, you may be able to use somewhat higher ratios."

Thus, you may find that if you make a 20 percent down payment, or agree to a higher rate of interest, the lender may allow the percentage of your income that goes for housing to be as large as 32 percent, and adjust the permissible total debt-to-income ratio upward. Be sure to ask what ratios the lender uses before applying for a loan.

Different Rules for "Jumbo" or "Nonconforming" Loans

In most areas of the country, a loan that conforms to Fannie Mae's requirements and is less than that institution's upper limit ($227,150 in 1998) will buy a very nice house. But suppose you're in a position to afford considerably more. "In that case," says Mitch Pomper, president of Newtown Financial Group, a Pennsylvania mortgage brokerage firm, "you'll need a so-called 'nonconforming' or 'jumbo' loan."

Like Fannie Mae–conforming loans, jumbos are also packaged and sold on the secondary market, and that market sets the desired ratios. "In general, the ratios are 33/38 for jumbo loans," Pomper says. "That's thirty-three percent of gross income for housing expenses and thirty-eight percent for total debt. The thought is that to qualify for a jumbo mortgage, you have to have a higher-than-average income. Since the cost of living represents a smaller percentage of that income than it does for Fannie Mae borrowers, the ratios are more generous. But increasingly, the market is relying on FICO scores. For borrowers with a high enough score, lenders will toss the ratios and make the loan."

FICO stands for First, Isaac & Company, the firm that developed the statistical models used by most of the leading credit bureaus. Also known as a *credit bureau score*, FICO is designed to quantify risk for the lender. It thus factors in items like your total indebtedness, the total amount of credit available to you, and whether you've been late paying any bills. You'll learn more about credit bureaus and how to get your own credit report later in this book.

In addition, special programs exist that offer more flexibility still. To make it easier for low- and moderate-income individuals to buy a home, some lenders will use Fannie Mae's Community Home Buyer's Program, which permits a housing expense ratio of 33 percent and a total debt-to-income ratio of 38 percent. (You'll learn more about such special programs later in this book.)

Where Do You Fit?
Median Home Prices and
Family Income

According to the National Association of Realtors, as of the end of the first quarter of 1998, the median price for an existing home was $127,000, while median household income in 1998 was projected to be about $45,000. (*Median* means half fall below those amounts and half are above.)

Both figures change slightly from quarter to quarter, and much depends on where you live. In mid-1998, for example, the median home price in San Francisco and Honolulu was close to $300,000, while in Syracuse, New York, it was about $80,000, and in Waterloo, Iowa, it was a bit over $65,000.

The same is true with household incomes. According to Metromail Corporation, a leading provider of direct-marketing products and services, New Jersey led the way in 1997 with a family median income of $66,500, Idaho was at $39,000, and Mississippi was at the bottom of the list at $32,900.

Finally, while you're pondering where you fit in this broad spectrum, it is worth noting that according to an annual survey by Chicago Title & Trust Company, the average first-time buyer is about thirty-two years old and in 1997 made an average down payment of 13.7 percent. The average repeat buyer is about forty-one years old and in 1997 made a 26.1 percent down payment. Repeat buyers, after all, have the appreciated value of their current homes on which to draw.

Doing the Math

Now that you have an idea of how a lender will look at you, and what lenders in general want to see when they do, you'll have the motivation to take the next step: calculating your net worth and drawing up a spending worksheet.

Both tasks can be a lot of work. You'll have to dig out documents, reconstruct spending patterns, and otherwise step back and do what your grandparents would refer to as "taking stock" of your financial life. There are two good reasons for investing the necessary time and effort, though.

First, you're going to have to do all this anyway when you apply for a loan. Second, there is no better way to get a sense of how buying a home will affect your lifestyle than by assembling a list of everything you are currently spending money on. Where does the money go? And where will it go after you buy a home? You don't have to answer those questions with scientific precision, but if you can't answer with a reasonable degree of confidence, you're not ready yet. Never forget that buying and owning a home, like raising a child, will always be more expensive than you expect.

What Are You Worth?

In banker's terms, net worth is the sum of your financial assets minus the sum of your financial liabilities. To put it more simply, it's the number you arrive at when you subtract the dollar value of what you owe from the dollar value of what you own.

Figuring your net worth will take some time. The worksheet provided in this chapter will be a big help, but you'll still have to assemble the information. Be sure to do this in a way that makes it easy to repeat the process in the future. (Many investment advisers recommend calculating your net worth once a year to measure the progress you've made in the previous twelve months.)

A box of manila folders and a filing cabinet (or a heavy-duty plastic or cardboard storage box from your local office-supply store) will help you get things organized. Computer programs like Quicken, Microsoft Money, and Managing Your Money have built-in forms for net-worth calculations, making it easy to perform the arithmetic and to keep your worksheets up to date.

How to Figure Your Net Worth

Use any system you like—the Net-Worth Worksheet provided on the following page, personal finance software if you have it, or simply a legal pad and pencil. You'll find the process to be an eye-opening exercise, particularly if you're thirty- or forty-something and have been working steadily since graduating from high school or college. For example, the assets in your checking and savings accounts are obvious. But what's the value of your 401(k) retirement plan? Your IRA or Keogh account? What about your pension, if you have one, or any stock options you may be fortunate enough to own?

Not only will the bank want this kind of information, you will too. For, as you'll learn later in this book, there's a very good chance you can bor-

SMART SOURCES

Personal finance programs are quite popular among personal computer users. In addition to helping you with household budgeting and net-worth calculations, such programs offer built-in loan amortization modules that prompt you for the loan amount, interest rate, and term and then quickly calculate your monthly payments. Here are the three leading packages and where to get more information about each:

Quicken
800-446-8848
www.quicken.com

Microsoft Money
800-426-9400
www.moneyinsider.
  msn.com

Managing Your Money
203-452-2600
www.mymnet.com

Net-Worth Worksheet

Assets

Checking Accounts
and Cash . . . . _____

Savings Accounts . . . . _____

IRA and Keogh Accounts _____

Stocks and Bonds . . . . _____

Mutual Funds . . . . _____

Pension and 401(k) Plans _____

Life Insurance Cash Value _____

Home . . . . _____

Other Real Estate . . . . _____

Personal Property
(cars, furniture, jewelry,
silver, furs, boats, tools,
collectibles) . . . . _____

Amounts Owed to Me
(loans and money due
for work already
performed) . . . . _____

Equity Value of
a Business . . . . _____

Other Assets

_____ . . . _____

_____ . . . _____

_____ . . . _____

Total Assets . . . . _____

Liabilities

Mortgages . . . . _____

Home Equity Loans . . . . . _____

Car Loans . . . . _____

Credit-Card Debt . . . . _____

Personal Loans . . . . _____

Student Loans . . . . _____

Other Loans . . . . _____

Taxes Owed

Income . . . . _____

Real Estate . . . . _____

Other . . . . _____

Other Liabilities

_____ . . . _____

_____ . . . _____

_____ . . . _____

Total Liabilities . . . . . _____

**Net Worth (Assets
minus Liabilities)**

row or withdraw (tax free) the money you need for your down payment from your retirement plan. It may or may not be the best option in your particular case, but it is definitely something you should know about.

Adding Up Your Assets

Fill in the easy stuff first—the balances in your checking and savings accounts and the latest numbers reported on your 401(k), IRA, and Keogh statements. Then move on to assets like your house (if you have one), cars, boats, a second home, other real estate holdings, and so on. What's their fair market value? In other words, what could you sell them for today? You'll also need to go from room to room in your house or apartment and create a list of personal possessions that are especially valuable—furniture, jewelry, antiques, collections, and so forth.

You don't have to be precise, but you have to be realistic. You may have paid $3,000 for a state-of-the-art personal computer a year ago, for example, but today it's worth considerably less and, of course, is no longer state of the art. On the other hand, that collection of antique dolls you inherited from your grandmother may be worth considerably more than you think.

Adding Up Your Liabilities

Now for the other side of the equation: what you owe. This is *not* the amount you pay to various creditors each month (the figure used earlier in this chapter to calculate your total debt-to-income ratio). Rather, it's your total debt. For example, in calculating your assets, you estimated what you could get for your car if you sold it today. On your liabilities list, you need to write down the outstanding balance on your car loan, since that balance would have to be paid off should you choose to sell your car. Note that if you lease your car, you do not own it, so it doesn't count as an asset, and your lease obligation does not count as a liability.

Total credit-card debt. Home-equity loan payments. Student loans. Income and real estate taxes that are due. Identifying your liabilities is rarely as challenging as identifying your assets. That's because creditors typically make a point of making themselves known to you.

Your Spending Worksheet: Where Does the Money Go?

"Getting and spending, we lay waste our powers," wrote William Wordsworth in his poem "The World Is Too Much with Us." But it is difficult to see how else one can live. We have to work for a living, and we also have to spend, though perhaps not as much as we do.

There are at least two good reasons for drawing up a budget-style spending worksheet as you begin to think about buying a house. First, you're going to need money for your down payment. You'll need more money still to cover closing costs and moving expenses. And then there are those "moving-in expenses," like drapes for the bedroom windows or new carpet for the family room. Your budget will help you get a clear idea of where your money goes each month and how to channel more of it into savings.

Visualizing Life in Your New Home

The second reason for performing this exercise is equally powerful: it will help you visualize life in your new home. You won't have rent payments anymore—you'll have mortgage payments. The money you're now spending on new clothes may have to be redirected to cover heat, water, and electric bills. Depending on your new location, you may spend more or less on gasoline and transportation. And, by the way, are you planning on having kids? If so, down the road you'll have all kinds of additional expenses, ranging from child care to braces to school costs.

On the plus side, you should find yourself paying less in federal income tax since interest payments on your mortgage are deductible. You won't be able to calculate how much less until you have a better idea of the amount of your mortgage, so you'll want to revisit your budget later.

When calculating the value of your mortgage-interest deduction, you should know that lenders

F.Y.I.

Prior to being outlawed in 1978, lead—because it was so durable—could be found in paint, plumber's solder, and even in water pipes. Now we know lead is dangerous, particularly to small children. So what do you do if you want to buy a pre-1978 home? You have it tested by a licensed inspector who will either use an X-ray process that does not disturb surfaces or collect actual chips of material.

If you have kids and if the home tests positive for lead contamination, you may have a number of options, ranging from removal to sealing or "encapsulation" of surfaces. Either way, lead removal and abatement is one of those expensive surprises you'd better plan for when working out your finances.

F.Y.I.

Children can have a major effect on how much house you can afford. The U.S. Department of Agriculture estimates that two-parent families with an average gross annual income of $46,100 spend $7,860 a year ($655 a month) raising a child from birth through age two. For those with average incomes of $87,300, the figure is $11,680 a year ($973 per month).

set things up so that most of your monthly payments for the first few years of a mortgage go to cover the interest. Thus you can pretty much just multiply your mortgage payment by 12, deduct the result from your taxable income, and look up the new amount in the tax tables. Real estate taxes are also deductible, but since they can vary so widely, you'll have to wait until you have a better idea of where you'll be living before including them.

Getting It All Down on Paper

The first step is to make a list of everything you spend money on in the course of a month. (For big, once-a-year items like vacations, lump-sum property taxes, or major purchases made during the year, divide the amount by 12.) Start with taxes. Then do home-related expenses like your mortgage or rent, phone, cable TV, water, gas, electric, maintenance, and repairs. Next, focus on clothing and food. And don't forget snacks and the coffee and bagel you buy on the train or at the office each morning.

Now that you're housed, clothed, and fed, think about recreation—movies (including the popcorn and soda), video rentals, books, magazines, newspapers, hobbies, pets, and all similar recreations.

Use the suggested expense categories in the Spending Worksheet provided on page 44 to get started. Then consult your checkbook and credit-card statements. Don't be too quick to complete this little exercise. In fact, you might want to return to your list several times during a typical week to record items that you missed.

Ready, Set, Calculate!

Now that you've assembled all of your financial and spending information, you're ready to calculate the amount of money the bank will probably be willing to lend you. Start by applying the housing expense ratio (28 percent) and the total debt-to-income ratio (36 percent) to your monthly gross (pre-tax) income. If you are applying for a jumbo loan (more than $227,150 in 1998), use a housing expense ratio of 33 percent and a debt-to-income ratio of 38 percent. For the sake of this example, we'll assume a household gross income from all sources of $60,000.

1. Divide your yearly household gross income by 12 to come up with your monthly gross income.

$60,000 ÷ 12 = $5,000 per month

2. Calculate the housing expense ratio by multiplying your monthly income by 0.28 (28 percent). The result will be the maximum monthly housing-cost payment, including PITI (principal, interest, taxes, and homeowner's insurance).

$5,000 x 0.28 = $1,400 (PITI max)

3. Calculate the total debt-to-income ratio by multiplying your gross monthly income by 0.36 (36 percent). The result will be the maximum total monthly debt payment, including PITI.

$5,000 x 0.36 = $1,800 (debt max)

Spending Worksheet

Expense Categories	Current Monthly Spending ($)	Possible Cuts ($)	Expense Categories	Current Monthly Spending ($)	Possible Cuts ($)
Taxes			Furniture and Appliances	_____	_____
Federal Income Tax	_____	_____	Maintenance and Repairs	_____	_____
Social Security and Medicare	_____	_____	*Food and Drink*		
State and Local Taxes	_____	_____	Groceries	_____	_____
			Restaurant Meals	_____	_____
Housing			Takeout	_____	_____
Mortgage or Rent	_____	_____	Beer, Wine, and Liquor	_____	_____
Property Taxes	_____	_____	*Clothes and Shoes*		
Gas, Electric, Heating Oil	_____	_____	Family Member 1:	_____	_____
Telephone	_____	_____	Family Member 2:	_____	_____
Cable TV	_____	_____	Family Member 3:	_____	_____
Water and Sewer	_____	_____	Family Member 4:	_____	_____
Trash Collection	_____	_____	Dry Cleaning	_____	_____
Cleaning Service and Supplies	_____	_____	Shoe Repair	_____	_____
Lawn Service	_____	_____			

Expense Categories	Current Monthly Spending ($)	Possible Cuts ($)	Expense Categories	Current Monthly Spending ($)	Possible Cuts ($)
Transportation			*Personal Care*		
Gasoline and Motor Oil	_____	_____	Haircuts	_____	_____
Car Maintenance and Repairs	_____	_____	Cosmetics and Toiletries	_____	_____
Tolls and Parking Fees	_____	_____	Health Club Membership	_____	_____
Public Transportation	_____	_____	*Health Care*		
			Doctor Visits	_____	_____
Recreation			Prescription Drugs	_____	_____
Books, Magazines, and Newspapers	_____	_____	Dental Care	_____	_____
Movies, Concerts, and Plays	_____	_____	Eye Care, Eyeglasses, and Contacts	_____	_____
Sports Events	_____	_____	Medical Supplies	_____	_____
Online Services	_____	_____	*Insurance*		
Hobbies	_____	_____	Home Owner's/ Renter's	_____	_____
Pets and Pet Care	_____	_____	Auto	_____	_____
Video/Audio Rentals	_____	_____	Life	_____	_____
Vacations and Travel	_____	_____	Health	_____	_____
			Disability	_____	_____
			Flood	_____	_____
			Earthquake	_____	_____

(continued)

Expense Categories	Current Monthly Spending ($)	Possible Cuts ($)	Expense Categories	Current Monthly Spending ($)	Possible Cuts ($)
Education			*Other Expenses*		
Tuition and Fees			Accountant	_____	_____
Books and Supplies	_____	_____	Bank Service Charges and Fees	_____	_____
Children			Charitable Contributions	_____	_____
Day Care and Baby-Sitters	_____	_____	Club Memberships	_____	_____
Toys and Playground Equipment	_____	_____	Credit-Card Memberships	_____	_____
After-School Activities	_____	_____	Gifts (Birthday, Holiday, etc.)	_____	_____
Debt Repayments			Legal Fees	_____	_____
Credit Cards	_____	_____	Other	_____	_____
Car Loans	_____	_____			
Home-Equity Loans	_____	_____	**Spending Totals**	_____	_____
Student Loans	_____	_____			

Monthly Cash Flow

Monthly Income
Salary (before taxes) . . . .   _____
Overtime Pay (before taxes) . . . .   _____
Bonuses and Commissions (before taxes) . . . .   _____
Investment Income (interest and dividends) . . . .   _____
Other Income . . . .   _____

Total Monthly Income . . . .   _____

Monthly Expenses (from Spending Worksheet) . . . . — _____

Monthly Surplus or Shortfall . . . .   [   ]

4. One of these two dollar amounts will be the limiting factor in what you can borrow, and you can use them in at least two ways. If you subtract the PITI max from the debt max, you'll discover just how low your nonmortgage debt payments—including credit cards, car loans, and the like—have to be to qualify for the PITI max.

$1,800 – $1,400 = $400 (total nonmortgage debt allowed)

5. Or you can subtract your actual nonmortgage debt from the debt max to learn the monthly mortgage payment the bank will allow. Assuming your nonmortgage debt is $800 a month in our example, the bank would want your PITI max to be no more than $1,000 a month.

$1,800 – $800 = $1,000

Putting It in Perspective

It is important to emphasize that there is flexibility in these ratios, so don't be discouraged by your results. If you're a first-time or minority buyer, you may be able to take advantage of special programs that use ratios of 30/40 or better. In addition, Fannie Mae and similar entities make allowances for local conditions and housing prices. And, of course, there are mortgage lenders who do not sell their loans to Fannie Mae or others and are not bound by their guidelines.

If you can make a down payment of 20 percent or better, if the property includes an income-producing rental unit, if the house is in an area with a history of rapid appreciation, and so on—there are lots of possibilities. Mortgage lending is not an exact science. In the end, lenders want to "sell" you their money. Otherwise, they make no profit. All they really care about is that they can count on you to repay them, and, should there be a problem, that their loan be secured by a property that can be sold at a price high enough to recoup any losses.

How Much Will the Bank Lend Me?

If you've made the 28/36 ratio calculations with your own gross monthly income figure, you now have some idea of what the bank would like to see in terms of the dollar amount of your monthly PITI payment. So how do you translate that into an actual loan amount? How do you use what you now know to estimate the size of the mortgage a lender will give you?

The first step is to strip out the tax and insurance components so that you're left with just principal and interest. Once that's done, you can use the resulting amount and the loan's interest rate to work backward to the mortgage amount.

Removing the tax and insurance components from the monthly payment can be tricky, largely because property taxes vary with the locality. You will want to contact a real estate agent or mortgage lending officer at a local bank for a more precise fix, but according to Century 21, one of the leading nationwide real estate chains, "As a rule of thumb, you can guess that about 20 percent of the housing expense will go for insurance and taxes and the remaining 80 percent for principal and interest."

Thus, continuing with our example, which assumes the bank will allow a PITI max of $1,000 a month, principal and interest would be $1,000 times 0.80 (80 percent), or $800. The question now is "If the monthly principal and interest payment is $800, what is the loan amount?"

A Bit of Simple Algebra

The approximate loan amount is easy to calculate once you know two things. First, you need to know the interest rate of the loan. Second, you need to be aware that virtually all of your first year's mortgage payments go for interest. That means that if you multiply your monthly principal and interest payment by 12, you will know the dollar total you will pay in interest in the first year. "Solving for" the mortgage amount is now quite easy.

How to Figure Your Mortgage Payment

There are several quick and easy ways to get a handle on monthly mortgage payments. You can use personal finance software packages like Quicken, Microsoft Money, or Managing Your Money, all of which include "mortgage calculator" features. Or you can use the mortgage calculator programs at various Web sites, including Fannie Mae (www.fanniemae.com), HSH Associates (www.hsh.com), and Bank Rate Monitor (www.bankrate.com).

If you don't have a computer, you can buy a book of amortization tables (or borrow one from the library). Or you can use the table shown here, which offers a brief subset of what you'd find in one of these books for a fixed-rate, 30-year loan at interest rates ranging from 6 to 10 percent.

Mortgage Payment Table

Monthly principal and interest for a fixed-rate 30-year loan

Loan Amount	6.0%	6.5%	7.0%	7.5%	8.0%	8.5%	9.0%	9.5%	10.0%
$ 10,000	$ 60	$ 63	$ 67	$ 70	$ 73	$ 77	$ 80	$ 84	$ 88
20,000	120	126	133	140	147	154	161	168	176
30,000	180	190	200	210	220	231	241	252	263
40,000	240	253	266	280	294	308	322	336	351
50,000	300	316	333	350	367	384	403	420	439
60,000	360	379	399	420	440	461	483	505	527
70,000	420	442	466	489	514	538	564	589	615
80,000	480	506	532	559	587	615	644	673	702

Loan Amount	6.0%	6.5%	7.0%	7.5%	8.0%	8.5%	9.0%	9.5%	10.0%
90,000	560	569	599	626	660	692	725	757	790
100,000	600	632	665	699	734	769	805	841	878
110,000	660	695	732	769	807	846	885	925	966
120,000	720	758	798	839	881	923	966	1,009	1,054
130,000	780	822	865	909	954	1,000	1,047	1,093	1,141
140,000	840	885	931	979	1,027	1,076	1,127	1,177	1,229
150,000	900	948	998	1,049	1,101	1,153	1,208	1,262	1,317
160,000	959	1,011	1,064	1,119	1,174	1,230	1,287	1,345	1,404
170,000	1,019	1,075	1,131	1,189	1,247	1,307	1,368	1,429	1,492
180,000	1,079	1,138	1,198	1,259	1,321	1,384	1,448	1,514	1,580
190,000	1,139	1,201	1,264	1,329	1,394	1,461	1,529	1,598	1,667
200,000	1,199	1,264	1,331	1,398	1,468	1,538	1,609	1,682	1,755
210,000	1,259	1,327	1,397	1,468	1,541	1,615	1,690	1,766	1,843
220,000	1,319	1,391	1,464	1,538	1,614	1,692	1,770	1,850	1,931
230,000	1,379	1,454	1,530	1,608	1,688	1,769	1,851	1,934	2,018
240,000	1,439	1,517	1,597	1,678	1,761	1,845	1,931	2,018	2,106
250,000	1,499	1,580	1,663	1,748	1,834	1,922	2,012	2,102	2,194

Note: For mortgages over $250,000, just add the appropriate figures. For example, to find the monthly mortgage payment for a $270,000 mortgage at 7.5%, add the amounts shown for $250,000 at 7.5% ($1,748) and $20,000 at 7.5% ($140) to get $1,888.

To put it another way:

Mortgage x Annual Interest Rate = Annual Interest Payment

So it follows that:
Mortgage = Annual Interest Payment ÷ Interest Rate

Using real numbers, if the monthly payment is $800, then the first year's total is 12 times $800, or $9,600. Assume an interest rate of 7.25 percent on a conventional 30-year loan, and crank those figures into the equation:

$9,600 ÷ 0.0725 = $132,413.79

Round it up to $133,000 for convenience.

What Price House Can I Buy?

If you have plugged in your own figures, you will have an idea of the size of the loan you can expect from a lender. As important as they are, though, these are rough, ballpark figures. Lots of variables can come into play. Still, you've got to start somewhere, so let's continue with the example.

If the bank will lend you $133,000, what price house should you be looking for? Keep in mind that you may not want to borrow the full amount the bank is willing to lend. Assume that you'll be making a 10 percent down payment. That means that $133,000 represents 90 percent of the price of the house. So, with just a bit more algebra, you can figure that the price of the house is about $148,000. (If $133,000 = 0.90x$, then $x = 133,000 \div 0.90$, or $147,777.)

Of course, house prices, like car prices, are negotiable. Only in a very hot real estate market do owners expect to get their full asking price. So someone expecting to actually sell a house for $148,000 would probably put it on the market with an asking price that is 7 to 10 percent more, in this case $158,000 to $163,000.

The Down Payment, Closing Costs, and Other Expenses

The mortgage amount is the largest part of a home-buying transaction. But since you will be paying it back over many years, you can probably find a way to manage the monthly payments, even if you have to cut back a bit on lifestyle expenses. And, the amount may not be much more than you're currently paying in rent.

Unfortunately, when it comes to estimating what you can afford, the devil really is in the details—the *immediate* details. For example, 10 percent of anything usually isn't very much. But, continuing with our example, to have to come up with a 10 percent down payment on a $148,000 house ($14,800)—right now!—can be a challenge for most people, no matter how much they earn.

And then there are the closing costs. You'll learn more about the specific costs involved later

"We were so young and naive," says Debbie, a computer software analyst at a major company in Washington, D.C. "We spent every nickel we had—and many that our parents gave us—getting into our first house. It was wonderful. All that space after five years of living in an apartment.

"Unfortunately, by the time we moved in, we had no money left for furniture. So we spent the first two years using our apartment furniture and rattling around in a bunch of empty rooms. We managed. But if I had it to do over again, I think I would have gone for less house and preserved more of our savings to spend on furniture and decorating."

in this book. What you need to know right now is that, according to Fannie Mae, closing costs can be from 3 to 6 percent of the mortgage amount. (Other authorities quote 2 to 5 percent of the *purchase* price.) So if you're borrowing $133,000, your closing costs can run from $4,000 to $8,000.

Leave Some Money for Contingencies

For the purposes of our example, let's assume that the closing costs will be in the middle of the range, or about $6,000. Add that to the 10 percent down payment of $14,800, and you're at $20,800. Some of this money you will have to pay out to bind the agreement and to make a deposit, but most of it you will have to pay out several weeks or months later at your closing.

At that point, you will have satisfied all your obligations under the transaction. You'll be handed the keys and be free to move in. Except, what if you don't have enough cash left to pay a mover or to rent a U-Haul and do it yourself?

What if you're moving into a home built prior to the mid-1970s that you know has lead paint? If your kids are at an age where everything goes into their mouths, and you don't have the money to have the lead paint removed, you'll have a major problem on your hands.

Or perhaps the previous owners had pets and the shag carpet in the family room literally stinks. Maybe they were heavy smokers and the only way to get rid of the smell is to repaint the interior. What if you want to have the random-width oak floors sanded and refinished in a darker color before you move in? And so on. There are moving costs and there are moving-in costs, and you'll need to have some money left over after you buy a house to cover both.

Good News (at Last!)

This is the bad news. The good news is that you do not necessarily have to make a 10 percent down payment. Thanks to government-insured loans, some banks will ask for only 3 to 5 percent down. Also, you may be able to roll most of the closing costs into your mortgage loan and thus pay them off over a longer period of time. Still, for best results, you should go into this process with eyes wide open. The next chapter will help you think about where you want to live and in what kind of dwelling. However, if you want to continue with the financial aspects of things, leap ahead to chapters 8 and 9 and learn all about the many options available for financing a home purchase.

Do not be discouraged. If you have a good credit record and at least two years of solid work history, you can almost certainly buy a home. There are programs available to help you secure a mortgage—lots of them. Just be realistic. Try to think beyond the mortgage and the closing costs to leave yourself some cash (not credit) to cover unexpected expenses.

THE BOTTOM LINE

The first step in determining how much home you can afford is to develop a clear picture of your net worth and your monthly spending habits. This will take some time, but you're going to have to do it anyway when you apply for a loan. You can use this information to get a rough idea of the size of the mortgage for which you qualify. Once you know how much you can borrow, you can get an idea of the kinds of houses and the price range at which you should be looking.

To avoid the classic home-buying mistakes, it is important to be realistic. So don't borrow more than you can *comfortably* repay, even if the bank is willing to lend it. It is also important to think ahead to closing costs, moving expenses, and moving-in expenses.

CHAPTER 4

....

Homes and Locations

One of the best collections of *Calvin and Hobbes* cartoons is titled *There's Treasure Everywhere*. But you don't have to be a fan of this little kid with his imaginary tiger friend Hobbes to appreciate the fact that there are *homes* everywhere as well. What you *do* have to do is free yourself from any preconceived notions about what constitutes a home.

Once you do this, you will see that there are indeed homes everywhere! They may not be quite what you imagined. They may not be anything like the wonderful home that Mom and Dad live in—the place that harbors fond memories, the place you go back to during the winter holidays. But a home can be yours, and it will help you begin to build equity.

How to Approach Home Buying

This is a distinctly unsentimental approach. But it is firmly rooted in financial realities. If you wait until you can afford a house like Mom and Dad's, or if you wait for a house to become available in a particular neighborhood, you will further postpone the day when you can stop throwing your money away on rent and start investing it instead.

No one is suggesting that you rush into anything or that you buy more house than you can comfortably afford. But when you're ready to buy, when the stars in your financial heavens are aligned, don't put the decision off because you can't find the "perfect" house. There *are* no perfect houses.

Buy quality. Buy a property that will appreciate. But buy *something!*

As long as you can see yourself living there for three to five years, you'll come out ahead. That is because after three to five years, the value of your dwelling will have—at the very least—increased enough to cover the closing costs that you paid when you bought it. More than likely, it will have increased enough to provide you with a substantial down payment on your next, even nicer, home.

None of this can happen if you continue to rent. So start planning today.

Thinking Long-Term

Of course, while the unexamined life may not be worth living, the overly planned life cannot be lived at all. Stuff happens, as everyone knows. Still, it doesn't hurt to have a general idea of where you hope to end up in the housing market. Your plan may go something like this:

An apartment in your mid-twenties. A two-bedroom bungalow in an established neighborhood in your early thirties. Followed by a bigger, highly desirable home in a new development (even if you hate orange-slice windows and think cathedral ceilings are a sinful waste of space), and then, after the kids are through college, a rambling old farmhouse on ten acres of land where you'll grow your own blueberries. Followed, of course, by the obligatory Sunbelt condo where you will spend your so-called golden years.

F.Y.I.

Today we take housing developments and subdivisions for granted. But prior to the creation of Levittown, New York, and Levittown, Pennsylvania—built in the late 1940s and early 1950s to house returning war veterans—individuals or couples would buy single lots and hire their own architects and builders to create their homes. By definition, every home was one of a kind.

Planning like this was a lot easier before the era of frequent job transfers and corporate downsizing. But it doesn't hurt to have a general outline in mind. And even if job transfers are your lot in life, there's no reason you can't plan to keep trading up each time you move, with your company picking up most of the normal moving expenses.

So, what are the possibilities? What kinds of dwellings can you own? And how can you evaluate the communities where they are located? Answering these questions is the focus of this chapter. In the next chapter, we'll zero in on how to assess and evaluate a given dwelling.

Single-Family Homes

In the musical *Little Shop of Horrors*, the female lead, Audrey, sings about wanting to move out of the city to live "someplace that's green." What she has in mind is a single-family detached home in the suburbs—which is to say, in a farmer's field that used to produce beets or sweet corn instead of houses filled with couples having children.

That was the ideal in the 1950s, and it is still the dream today. A brand-new single-family home with lots of bedrooms, lots of bathrooms, a "media room," and an incredible country kitchen. And pay no attention to those twiglike saplings at the front of the house. In a few years, they will grow into the most amazing array of sugar maples, offering deep shade in summer and brilliant colors in the fall. In just a year or two you will never suspect that this neighborhood used to be a cow pasture.

Variations

A brand-new house in a suburban housing development is only one form of detached single-family home. There are many variations, each with its own pluses and minuses. For example, you may not like living in a development where every fourth house looks the same because the builder used a limited number of designs. You might be happier in an older development in which the growth of vegetation and changes made by various owners have made it far less obvious that there are really only a few basic floor plans.

For more uniqueness still, there are entire neighborhoods of custom-built homes. These tend to be older, which can be good if interior details like real plaster walls and more substantial wood trim are important to you. But they can be less than good if they require a lot of maintenance and remodeling to make them suitable to your needs.

Or you might want to consider building your own home. You may see empty lots offered by contractors with signs reading "Will build to suit," for example. Or you may find a lot, buy it, and hire your own builder. If that's too expensive, you might have a contractor dig a foundation and purchase a factory-built "manufactured" house for it. (In some areas of the country, manufactured homes cost up to 50 percent less than site-built houses.) If you're really adventurous (and handy), you might even consider a precut home like a log cabin that will arrive in pieces for you to assemble at the site.

As you can see, there are lots of single-family-home possibilities. And you can be sure that these are only just the beginning.

Condos and Town Houses

Condominiums and town houses are often more affordable than detached houses. And because each involves a form of shared ownership, they typically offer the low-maintenance lifestyle of apartment living combined with the tax and equity-building advantages of buying a home. On the downside, housing of this sort does not appreciate as rapidly, and it is not as easy to sell as a single-family house.

Condominiums

The typical condominium is an apartment in a multi-unit structure. The interior of the apartment is privately owned, while the grounds, hallways, parking lots, swimming pools, and tennis courts are owned in common. The ownership mechanism for the common areas is usually a corporate entity like a homeowners association with officers and a board elected by everyone in the development.

Town Houses

Town house developments generally follow the condominium ownership model. But there are some important structural differences to note. Town houses are usually multi-floor, vertical units that share a common wall with one or two neighboring units.

Condo and Town House Pros and Cons

Pros

• No external maintenance (lawn mowing, leaf raking, snow shoveling, painting, and such).

• Access to pools, tennis courts, club-house facilities, and golf courses owned by the complex.

• Usually less expensive to buy and maintain than a detached single-family home.

• Tax and equity-building benefits that are equivalent to buying a home.

Cons

• Monthly maintenance fees.

• Little or no freedom in landscaping, external paint colors, window treatments, and even interior alterations in some complexes.

• Vulnerability to special assessments for major repairs to the complex (roofs, resurfacing the parking lot, among others).

• Generally sluggish appreciation and less easy to sell than a house.

These are more like a house than an apartment. And because there is no one above or below you, you own both the ground beneath the unit and the rights to the air above it. Usually, the homeowners association (and your monthly maintenance fees) will take care of the front of your town house, but responsibility for maintaining the backyard (if there is one) may rest with you.

Big City Option: Co-Ops

Still another form of housing ownership is the cooperative apartment building or co-op. Found

"When shopping for a condo or a town house," says Century 21 real estate expert Arnie Neumann (arnie@drcca.com), "make sure you know exactly what your monthly fee covers. Some complexes are more efficiently run than others and therefore have lower fees.

"Also, try to avoid complexes that include all utilities in the fee. This is the most expensive way to pay for utilities. That's because the fee is set to cover the most wasteful users. You could be subsidizing the people who waste electricity and heat. Try to find units that are individually metered so you can pay your own—and no one else's—utilities."

mainly in large cities like New York and Chicago, co-ops are corporations that hold title to an apartment building. As a resident, you own two things: shares in the corporation and a proprietary lease granting tenancy in a specific unit in the building. You thus occupy—but do not own—the unit.

Shareholders pay a pro-rated share of the corporation's expenses (mortgage, taxes, maintenance, etc.), and they can take a tax deduction for their share of the taxes and interest the corporation pays. The shares of stock can be assigned or sold, but the proprietary lease is usually severely restricted. The co-op board typically decides who can and cannot live in the building.

Location Matters

Anyone who believes that artificially intelligent computers will ever replace human beings need only try buying a house. The details and trade-offs that must be weighed when considering the various *types* of housing available could bring a supercomputer to its knees. And now you must add the matter of *location*. The old saying about the essence of real estate boiling down to just three things, all of them the L-word, will not be repeated here. But there is simply no question that *where* your house, condo, or town house is located can be of considerable importance.

For example, if you have school-age children, you will want to make sure your dwelling is in a good school district. For others, real estate taxes and even local, city, or township income taxes may be the determining factors. And how will you and your spouse commute to your respective jobs?

What's the community like? Surprising as it may be, even in big cities like New York, there are blocks and neighborhoods that have developed a sense of community far stronger than can be found in many suburban developments. How important is the flavor and closeness of your community, whether you live in the city or in the suburbs?

Where You're Coming From

If you will be buying within, say, a fifty-mile radius of where you grew up, you'll have the advantage of knowing the area. You and your parents, grandparents, and friends will know the good neighborhoods and the good schools. You and they will be familiar with local issues, politics, taxes, environmental hazards, planned development, and more.

If you're being transferred into a new area, there is no way you can know it as thoroughly as a long-time resident. But then, you really don't have to. The market—the prices people are paying for housing in various locations—will identify the prime areas for you. If comparable houses in different locations are selling for prices that are 10 to 15 percent or more apart, there has to be a reason. Which is to say: More than likely, the locals know something you don't—or have yet to discover.

You can't rely on just one transaction, of course, since any given sale may be skewed up or down. The owner may have been eager to sell and thus priced the house below the market, or a naive buyer may have overpaid for a given property. Be sure to consider several actual sales in each neighborhood before forming an opinion.

F.Y.I.

House and land sales are a matter of public record, so regardless of the location, you can always find out exactly how much a given property was sold for. Check with the Register of Deeds, or its equivalent, at the county courthouse. Recent real estate transactions are also usually published in local newspapers.

House Hunting on the Internet

The Internet can be a powerful tool for identifying both locations and homes that meet your criteria. You can get information on the median income in a particular area, the quality of the schools, and neighborhood crime rates. And you can search for a home by type, number of bedrooms, bathrooms, square footage, and other characteristics such as price range, age, and amenities like hardwood floors, swimming pools, and amount of land.

There are some caveats, however. The search software and user interface at some sites is better than others, and not all sites offer the same collection of features. More important, the number of homes listed varies widely. One site might have 400,000 listings, for example, while another has 1.5 million. The disparity is due to the differing policies of local real estate associations regarding releasing multiple listing service (MLS) data to online services. Such differences may be resolved in the future. In the meantime, you'll want to check several or all of the following Web sites to find the ones offering what you need:

CyberHomes
www.cyberhomes.com

HomeShark
www.homeshark.com

HomeAdvisor
homeadvisor.msn.com

Realtor.com
www.realtor.com

An Agent in Every Town

Another good idea for those moving in from out of town or out of state is to work with two or more real estate agents. Real estate agents tend to be most familiar with the housing stock available in their own immediate areas, so if you're considering two towns twenty-five miles apart, make a point of establishing a relationship with an agent in each town.

You're not "cheating on" anyone by doing this. As this book vigorously points out, real estate agents don't work for you, they work for the seller. And they don't make a dime until they sell you something. So forget about the fact that the agent in Town A will happily sell you a home a hundred miles away in Town B (and happily collect a commission). He or she can't know Town B nearly as well as Town A, so you will be better off establishing a relationship with an agent local to Town B.

Evaluating Locations

For most people, the three most important location-related considerations are these: the length of the commute to and from work, the quality of the schools, and the likely resale value of the house several years from now. There are many other things to think about as well, but you'll go crazy if you try to deal with them all at once, so just start with these.

As you begin to evaluate a location on these and other points, it is crucial to take a proactive approach. Don't assume anything. Verify every important detail yourself. If you're told that the commute is just fifteen minutes, try it yourself during rush-hour conditions. If you're told that the big field across the way has been set aside as a "green space" that can never be built upon, contact the proper authorities to verify the status of the land. If you're told that it's a quiet neighborhood, go spend some time driving around at different hours of the day. It may be that things are not quiet at all when people are home from work and kids are out of school.

Commuting

No one wants to spend a lot of time traveling to and from work every day. But everyone wants a spacious, comfortable house in a crime-free neighborhood with a good school system and other amenities. Since you are not likely to find such a place near a factory or industrial park, and since you may not be able to afford it in the city, you and your mate will probably have to commute.

So do this: Assume that a distance of twenty miles is equal to a half-hour commute and use a map of the area and a draftsman's compass to lay out a circle around your job location with a radius equal to twenty miles. Then look at the names of the towns near the circumference of your circle.

There's no need to be precise. Indeed, if your part of the country has good mass-transit service, you can probably draw a bigger circle. The goal is to give yourself a starting point and to identify some locations you may never have thought about. If you can't find what you want within this circle, you may have to accept a longer commute.

Location: Points to Consider

In addition to the commute, the schools, and future resale value, consider the following when evaluating a location:

• Proximity to parks, swimming pools, tennis courts, golf courses, and other recreational facilities.

• Convenience of airports.

• Quality and location of local libraries.

• Houses of worship.

• Day-care providers and baby-sitters.

• Shopping facilities.

• Proximity to family, friends, and relatives.

• Environmental hazards and industrial pollution.

• Local crime rate (ask the police).

• Future development (check with local planning commission).

Schools

It is certainly encouraging to hear a real estate agent say, "Centerville has a good school system." But that statement alone is worthless. It is much better to know that the mean SAT score for Centerville High was 1,200 last year. That's a verifiable fact, not an opinion. Performance data of this sort is available from school principals and district administrators. And if it isn't, you should ask why not.

You should also make a point of visiting the school or schools your kids will attend. Talk to the teachers and administrators. Ask about crime, violence, and drug problems. You might even want to attend the next meeting of the parent-teacher organization and try to develop your own sense of the school, its programs, and its teachers.

Also, be aware that just because you will have a Centerville mailing address doesn't necessarily mean that your kids will go to Centerville schools. Go to the district offices and ask to see the map showing the district's boundaries. Be particularly cautious if the house is located on or near one of those boundaries. If Elm Street is the boundary, it could be that kids on one side of the street will go to Centerville, while those on the other side are in a different, less desirable district.

Resale Value

The resale value of your home will depend on demand and desirability. Demand can be defined as the number of people who want to buy houses in your area. There's not much you can do to increase demand, but you can certainly do your best to avoid

SMART SOURCES

Lots of data is collected on local schools by organizations like the College Board, the Department of Education, and school districts themselves. A company called SchoolMatch collects and analyzes this data and makes the results available to interested parents for a small fee (usually about $40 per report). SchoolMatch reports are especially helpful to those being transferred, and many companies offer its services to their transferees free of charge. For more information, contact:

SchoolMatch
5027 Pine Creek Drive
Westerville, OH 43081
800-992-5323
www.schoolmatch.com

locations where demand could significantly drop in the future. For example, "one-horse towns" that depend on a single industry or company for most of the area's jobs are far more vulnerable than those with a mixed economy. Should the jobs disappear, so will the demand for housing.

You have considerably more control over the desirability of your house. For example, even if you don't have kids, buying a home in a good school district will make it desirable to buyers in the future. And, of course, budget permitting, you can add features to your home that will make it more desirable than many others.

Use Your Imagination

When it comes to deciding where and in what you want to live, the biggest mistake you can make is to be complacent. Buying a home is a big step. It is no time to just take things as they come or to accept at face value everything that people tell you. If you want to be happy with the results of the home-buying process, you have to *engage*. You have to invest your time, energy, and effort.

It's also a good idea to use your imagination. Free yourself from all your preconceptions about what constitutes a home. Once you do this, you will discover that there are homes everywhere, and every one of them will help you build equity. It is equally important to use your imagination when considering locations. Go to the local library, for example, and read a few back issues of the local newspaper. If you think you might like to live in the area, consider subscribing to the paper for a few months.

If you have access to the Internet, use a search engine such as AltaVista (www.altavista.com) or Yahoo! (www.yahoo.com) to look for any Web sites put up by the community, city, or town you're considering. And when you've identified a desirable spot and want to look at houses there, instead of staying in a hotel, consider staying in a bed-and-breakfast in the area to get a better feel for what it would be like to live there.

THE BOTTOM LINE

If you've always lived in one kind of house or apartment, you're probably not aware of all the other housing opportunities that exist. For example, if you grew up in a detached, single-family home, you may never have considered buying a duplex in which you live in one half and rent out the other. The key thing is to be open-minded and flexible.

The same is true when considering locations. Don't automatically rule anything out. Instead, take the time and make the effort to identify and get to know the possibilities. Take nothing for granted, nothing as a given. Instead, use your energy and imagination to get to know a spot before you buy a house there.

Real Estate Agent Options

Few people perform surgery, file a lawsuit, conduct a funeral, or buy a home every day. Given the complexity of these activities, it's easy to understand why most people turn to professionals. Less obvious is the formal and informal control these specialists have established over their respective professions.

For example, there is no law requiring a real estate agent to charge the seller a commission of 5 to 7 percent of the sale price of a home, yet if you question the commission percentage, most real estate agents will try to give you the impression that the rate is all but statutory. In reality, commissions are like nearly every other aspect of a real estate deal—completely negotiable. This directly affects you as the buyer, for the less the seller has to pay in commissions, the less you'll have to pay the seller.

To put it another way, many real estate agents will cut their commission percentage to make a deal go through. They don't want you to know this, but it's true. That's why you need to understand your options and how the game is played—precisely what you will learn here.

Three Ways to Go

When you buy a home you participate in a process involving customs and procedures that date back hundreds, even thousands, of years. Titles, deeds, mechanic's liens, encumbrances, disputed or inaccurate survey boundaries, and long-forgotten easements are as old as civilization—but as current as anything you'll encounter today. And encounter them you will.

That's why most people need professional help of some sort when dealing with such matters. As a prospective home buyer, once you have identified desirable locations, you have three main choices: go it alone, work with a real estate agent, or hire a buyer's broker.

The only reason to go it alone is if you are buying a property offered "for sale by owner"—FSBO (pronounced "fizz-bo") in trade talk. With no real estate agent involved on either side, there will be no commission to pay. However, both you and the seller will definitely want to hire attorneys who specialize in real estate to handle the legal aspects of the transaction.

Brokers and Agents

As noted, commissions may be negotiable. But because of the way the real estate industry has been organized by its members, it is very difficult to avoid paying one and still have lots of houses to choose from. The two terms to know here are *broker* and *agent.* Both positions require individuals to take courses and to pass separate state licensing exams.

The broker owns the firm and may be an individual, a corporation, or a partnership. The broker's salespeople must be individuals. Those salespeople, of course, are the real estate agents, and they cannot sell anything unless they are associated with a broker. (Real estate professionals who use the designation *Realtor* or *Realtor-Associate* are simply brokers and salespeople who are members of the National Association of Realtors, a trade association that promotes professional ethics and lobbies for the interests of the industry.)

The broker provides salespeople with a desk, a phone, and clerical services. Brokers also pay for newspaper ads and other expenses associated with

F.Y.I.

According to career information publisher The Princeton Review, after five years of experience, the typical real estate agent has an annual income of $34,300. After ten to fifteen years of experience, agents average about $49,000. Assuming that an agent's commission averages about 2.25 percent, to earn $49,000, an agent must sell $2.2 million of real estate. That's about seventeen properties at $130,000 each, or about nine at $250,000.

SMART SOURCES

How can you evaluate a real estate broker? A free publication called *Real Estate Brokers* from the federal government can help. It offers a wealth of information on what the law requires for real estate brokers, consumer rights and responsibilities, and the steps to take if you believe you've been unfairly treated. For a copy, write or call:

Federal Trade
   Commission
Public Reference
   Room, Room 130
Washington, D.C.
   20580-0001
202-326-2222

selling a property. In return, they typically receive half of the commission the real estate agent collects on each sale.

For their part, agents have two main jobs: to get listings and to show and sell properties. Real estate agents make a point of knowing lots of people so that when those people want to buy or sell a house, they already have a relationship. When they list with a brokerage, sellers sign an agreement giving the broker the exclusive right to list the property for a set period of time.

Multiple Listing Services

Of course, any real estate agent can show you and sell you any house, regardless of which broker has the listing. That's because almost all brokers belong to a multiple listing service (MLS) of some sort. These are local organizations whose broker members have agreed to share their listings. Members have also agreed on how sales commissions should be split.

In most cases, the commission is a total of 6 percent of the sale price. And it is usually paid by the seller. If the agent who got the listing for the broker also makes the sale, the agent and the broker usually each get 3 percent. (This is a powerful incentive for any given agent to try to sell you the properties he or she has listed.) If some agent associated with another brokerage sells the property, both the selling agent and the listing agent typically get 3 percent, which they must then split with their respective brokers.

Certainly customs, procedures, percentages, and splits differ across the country, but this is generally the way things work. And, as noted, it is the seller who pays the commission. This means that, contrary to what 70 percent or more of home buyers believe (according to Federal Trade Commission surveys), your real estate agent does *not* work for you. He or she works for the seller. It also means that it is in the agent's best financial interests to get you to pay the highest price possible for a given property.

What Your Broker Won't Tell You

SmartMoney.com, "the *Wall Street Journal* magazine of personal business," has a lot to offer any prospective home buyer, including "Ten Things Your Broker Won't Tell You." Here we'll summarize five of those things that pertain to buyers, but to look at the complete article, point your Web browser at the SmartMoney Answer Center at www.smartmoney.com/ac/home.

• "You're the only bidder on this house."
If an agent says you'd better hurry because there are other bidders for the property, ask to see the other bids. That information is supposed to be confidential, but if other offers really exist, in some cases the agent will show them to you.

• "You should be using more than one agent."
There's nothing to stop you from seeing homes with more than one agent. And if you're looking in a large geographic area, you'll need more than one agent to make sure that you have access to all of the multiple-listing services in those places.

• "Here is what you need to know about this house."
Real estate agents have a legal obligation to pro-

SMART SOURCES

The Internet and the World Wide Web have already begun to have an impact on the home-sales industry. Most savvy brokers have put up regularly updated Web sites that let you search for properties by nearly any criterion you can imagine. But so, too, have "for sale by owner" folks. So check out the Abele Owners' Network at www.owners.com.

Here you'll be able to search for FSBO homes by state, county, price range, number of bedrooms, and much more. At this writing, only about fifty thousand homes are listed (compared to the hundreds of thousands of homes listed nationwide). But this is really only the beginning of "cyber home sales—by owner."

SMART MONEY

Don't reveal the highest price you will pay to your real estate agent. That's the advice of *SmartMoney* magazine. "As you begin to drive around town with seasoned agents, you'll quickly find that they act like they are, in fact, working for you. So don't get too cozy. You will probably be tempted to tell an agent the highest price you are willing to pay for a house or the size of down payment you can afford. Don't. The agent is obligated to pass those details on to the seller, which could hurt you in negotiations."

You should also be aware that close relationships often exist between real estate agents and mortgage originators, loan officers, and title insurance companies, in which the latter pay referral fees to the agent for steering business their way.

tect any confidential information, such as the seller's absolute lowest price or the fact that the couple selling the house might be going through a divorce and thus may be looking for a quick deal. Nor do they have to draw your attention to any structural defects or similar problems.

• "I might use whatever you tell me against you."
If you tell the agent the highest price you will actually pay for a house or that your company will pay closing costs as part of your transfer package, the agent must by law pass on this information to the seller.

• "I'm pushing my own listings."
A given real estate agent can make much more money if he or she is both the listing agent (the person who persuaded the sellers to list the property with his or her agency) and the selling agent (the person who actually closes the deal). At the very least, this can represent a potential conflict of interest when it comes to finding you a home.

Buyer's Brokers

Finally, depending on where you live, you may have the option of hiring a *buyer's broker* (or *buyer's agent*). Unlike the traditional real estate agent who works for the seller, a buyer's broker represents you in the purchase of a house. These professionals do everything a traditional agent does—indeed, most are traditional real estate agents. The difference is that they are motivated and legally obligated to look out for *your* best interests. (There are buyer's broker–only firms, but, more and more, conventional real estate offices are offering "buyer's agency/brokerage" options, so be sure to ask.)

A buyer's broker may be paid a percentage of the sale price, a fixed fee, an hourly rate, or a combination of all three. (Most multiple listing services today require members to agree to split commissions with buyer's brokers just as they do with agents serving the seller.) According to *Money* magazine, "Buyers average a 5 percent savings when represented by a buyer's agent rather than a sales agent." The main drawback is that you will probably be required to sign an agreement requiring you to use a given buyer's broker exclusively for a set period of time. But then, most buyers find themselves working with the same conventional real estate agent without ever signing a similar agreement.

The Real Estate Buyer's Agent Council (REBAC) is the largest association of real estate professionals focusing on this area. For the name of a buyer's broker in your area, call them at 800-648-6224, or visit the REBAC Web site at www.rebac.net.

According to REBAC, the benefits of hiring a buyer's agent or broker include:

• Exclusive representation. Complete loyalty without conflicts of interest.

• Confidentiality concerning your money and motivation.

• Unbiased showing of all available homes whether listed with a brokerage or offered by owners.

• Information and advice about the property, including flaws that no "conventional" agent would point out.

F.Y.I.

State-protected ownership of private property is one of the underpinnings of civilization. It was the need to reestablish property markers after the annual flood of the Nile that prompted the Egyptians to develop mathematics. In the first draft of the Declaration of Independence, the famous phrase read, "life, liberty, and the pursuit of property," not "happiness." And, at the risk of dashing childhood illusions, the "plum" little Jack Horner pulled out of the pie was not a fruit but a property deed to a very fine manor owned by Abbot Whiting at the time Henry VIII was taking over English churches and monasteries.

• Disclosure of everything an agent knows or can discover.

• Hassle-free relocation—your interests and timetable are foremost.

• A fair and straightforward buyer agency agreement.

• An agent/agency that gets the job done right with no surprises

• Assistance in determining if a property is overpriced, advice about offering less than the asking price, and information about the seller's motivation. This information is not available from a seller's agent.

• Help in finding good home inspectors, lenders, and information.

Getting Smart about Commissions

Hiring a buyer's broker may be the most economical way to buy a house. But if no one is available in your area or if you find yourself socially obligated to work with an agent who happens to be a personal friend, it is worth thinking about commissions.

Naturally, you don't want to hammer a personal friend. But several thousand dollars is serious money in anyone's book, so from the very beginning you might want to discuss the topic of commissions with whomever you select. And rest assured that if you don't bring it up, your real estate agent friend won't either.

The notion that the real estate agent's sales commission doesn't enter into a seller's calculations when setting the price is as foolish as the idea that the cost of TV ads for breakfast cereals isn't folded into the price you pay for the stuff at the supermarket. Yet advertising agencies and real estate agents would have you believe otherwise.

Is This Fair?

Everyone needs to make a living. Everyone should be fairly compensated for the work they do. But is this fair? Assuming a rate of 6 percent, the brokerage commission on a $130,000 house is $7,800. On a house that costs twice as much ($260,000), the dollar amount of the commission is also doubled, to $15,600. If the house sold for $325,000, the commission would be $19,500.

Does it actually cost a real estate brokerage $7,800 more to sell a $260,000 house than a $130,000 house? Do the brokers run more newspaper ads or hold more open houses? And just how did the brokers and agents involved manage to spend nearly $20,000 marketing that $325,000 house?

If real estate brokers actually held the inventory—if they bought the homes from the owners and incurred interest and carrying charges commensurate with the prices they paid—then charging a flat percentage, regardless of the home's price, might make sense. But this is not the case. The commission percentage is the same, regardless of the price, though the actual dollar amounts earned can be significantly different.

STREET SMARTS

Real estate columnist Ilyce Glink had a personal encounter with the problems that can occur because a real estate agent really works for the seller. "I once went with my sister-in-law to look at some property in Boston," she writes. "We went to see several condominiums. Each one had several obvious flaws. In one, a particularly noticeable water stain covered most of the ceiling in the bedroom. The agent never said a word as he showed us the space. Finally I asked him about the water stain. 'I'm not sure what that is,' he said. I asked him what price he would pay for the property. 'Full price,' he said. [His answer was] by the book. Conventional brokers . . . are not required to tell you about any defects you can see with the naked eye, and they may only have to disclose structural defects if you ask about them."

In addition, few brokerages make any kind of written commitment to a seller about the marketing steps they will take to sell the home. They will do the best they can, but they don't say they will pay for a specific number of ads in the real estate section of the Sunday paper, distribute brochures, or run ads on cable TV. And, of course, there is no penalty if a brokerage firm fails to sell a property. Should that happen, the broker and the sales agents forgo a commission, but there are always plenty of other properties on the market.

Selecting a Real Estate Professional

Whether you opt for a traditional real estate agent who acts as a buyer's broker or someone who acts on behalf of the seller, you will want to take the time to choose the individual carefully. Probably you shouldn't use a close personal friend who is in the business. You may also not even want to use an acquaintance for such an important financial transaction. Remember, as part of the process of "qualifying" you as a serious buyer, the real estate agent will want you to submit information regarding your income, debt, and savings, something you may not feel comfortable doing with a friend or acquaintance.

So assume for the moment that you don't know anyone in the business. What do you do? Start by calling the local board of realtors and asking for the names of the agents who sold the most property in the last year. Most local boards present awards to agents based on the total dollar value of the property they've sold and the number of actual sales transactions.

It's almost impossible to earn such awards working part-time, so the individuals who do earn them clearly take their profession seriously and really work at it. That's what you want—someone who will actively search for a home that meets your criteria.

Next, make a point of interviewing several of these top-ranked agents. You want someone with whom you are compatible. Someone who listens and who can almost instinctively grasp your needs. You also want someone who remembers what you've seen and what you liked and disliked about each house.

It may also be a good idea to consult friends, family, and business associates. And, if you're interested in a home that's a little different from the run-of-the-mill, check the real estate ads in the Sunday paper. You may find that some brokerages specialize in relatively new "executive homes" in developments or in-town row houses or antique "country" homes. Again, any agent you select can sell you any home. But a brokerage that specializes in one particular kind of property is likely to have agents who are very familiar with that part of the market.

Finally, check the paper for weekend open houses for the kind of properties you want. Usually the agent who listed the property will be there as host. This is an excellent opportunity to informally interview that individual. Be sure to inquire what that person thinks of buyer's agents or buyer's brokers and, if you sense that you might hit it off, whether he or she can, and would want to, serve in that role for you.

THE BOTTOM LINE

Buying a home, like purchasing any piece of property, is a common, but complex, procedure. So even if you opt to go it alone, you will need the services of an experienced real estate attorney. More than likely, however, you'll also want to use a real estate professional.

The key things to remember are, first, that in the traditional relationship, the real estate agent works for and is responsible to the seller. Second, in many locations you can hire an agent to work for you as a buyer's agent or broker. And third, like everything else in real estate, the commission you agree to pay or any other form of compensation is completely negotiable. So don't be shy. Failing to raise this issue could cost you thousands of dollars.

Evaluating Properties

There are any number of stories in the real estate industry of rich clients buying a property because they love the location and then leveling the house to make room for a dwelling of their own design. Nothing wrong with that, but most people don't have the dollars to do it. Instead, they identify two or three locations/neighborhoods in an area (as discussed in chapter 4) and then begin narrowing the focus to what kind of housing is available in those areas.

But once the options have been identified, how do you zero in on and begin to evaluate and compare specific structures? That's the focus of this chapter. As you will see, you are perfectly qualified to do many initial evaluations yourself, once you know what to look for. However, once you start to get really serious about a given property, you will want to bring in a certified inspector/engineer. And, should that individual identify serious problems, you may want to take the further step of bringing in a specialist.

On Your Own: First Impressions

Everyone has heard the expression "Home is where the heart is." *Bartlett's Familiar Quotations* is filled with similarly affectionate references to "home." So clearly, buying the house, town house, condo, or co-op that is to become your home is an emotional issue. The real estate industry knows this and so, just as in the automotive industry, its members will do everything they can to appeal to your emotions.

These folks are just doing their jobs, but as a consumer, you need to be aware that while a good real estate agent may be genuinely interested in your children when he or she asks you about what they like to do, a really good agent will file those facts away and bring them out when showing you a home. "Oh, Kira and Sean would have such fun in this playroom, and it's so isolated that you'll never hear the noise."

Yes, and it may not be heated either, so they won't be able to use it during the winter unless you install an expensive heating system. The agent is under no obligation to point out this little "defect." But should you be alert enough to notice it yourself, the agent may say, "Well, yes, but an inexpensive electric space heater will do the trick. Sears had one on sale just last week."

In sales training this is called "overcoming objections." A good real estate salesperson will help you visualize yourself and your family in a given house, feed your imagination with possibilities based on what the salesperson knows about you, and quickly offer a solution should you raise a doubt or objection (probably because the salesperson was well aware of the problem and had already prepared an answer should you notice it as well).

Ignore Your Feelings

Your job is to be polite but to disconnect your hot buttons. Let the real estate agent do his or her best, but ignore it all. Soak up the impressions, ask to be allowed to walk through the house on your own, and as you are leaving and the agent says, "Well, what do you think?" be completely

F.Y.I.

According to the Urban Land Institute report *America's Real Estate* (202-624-7096, www.uli.org), the median age of an American home is now thirty years, and about 45 percent of homes have been built since 1970. The average home contains between five and six rooms, including a full bath and kitchen. Spending on housing and household operations now constitutes 26 percent of total personal income (national average). The average rate of increase in the price of a standard 10,000-square-foot lot is about 6 percent a year, nearly twice the rate of inflation in recent times.

noncommittal (even if you are in love with the house). Once again, the real estate agent works for the seller, and is obligated to keep that person informed, so don't reveal anything!

Give yourself and your significant other, if he or she is involved, time to let the dust settle. No human being can possibly absorb and assimilate all the features, possibilities, and pluses and minuses of a house instantaneously. And remember this: If someone is pressuring you to make a quick decision, you should probably back away. Do not listen to what some salesperson says about how many houses in a development have been sold or spoken for. If the houses are in such demand, that fact will show up in the actual sales transactions. So ask the developer to produce the committal letters, contracts, and photocopies of deposit checks, or to simply identify the specific properties that have sold in the last three months. Then verify the sales at the county courthouse.

What to Look For

Every dwelling has what real estate professionals refer to as "curb appeal." This is simply the first impression a house makes from the street. Savvy home owners and real estate agents will plant flowers, trim bushes and trees, give the driveway a fresh coat of sealant, and take other steps to enhance the curb appeal of a house before putting it on the market. This is all to the good, for it means that you can make the house look at least as attractive should you buy it.

Exterior Details

Your real estate agent will probably want to get you inside immediately, but if you can manage it, pause a moment to look at the house from the outside. You don't have to be trained in architecture to tell whether a house is well designed. Just ask yourself the following questions:

• Does the house have a unity of style? Do the details look as though they go together?

• How many building materials have been used? Brick and clapboard or stucco and clapboard mesh well, but a house of brick, clapboard, stucco, and fieldstone is likely to look like a mish mash.

• Are the doors, windows, dormers, and other details in proportion? Balance and symmetry can be as important in a house as in a work of art.

• Do the roofline and walls give a sense of unity and flow? Houses with lots of corners in their rooflines or walls that make twists and turns can look chopped up.

Again, what you're looking for is good design. Remember, a house or an addition to a house doesn't just happen. Someone, somewhere had to sit down and decide "what goes where." As in everything else, some people are better at this than others.

The Seven Most Common Floor-Plan Flaws

1. Front door opens directly into living room.

2. Bedroom or bathroom clearly visible from living room or main entryway.

3. Lack of eating area in or adjoining the kitchen.

4. Formal dining room too far from kitchen.

5. Excessive number of doors and/or windows in a room, making furniture placement a design challenge.

6. Interior gas, water, or electric meters requiring meter readers to enter the house.

7. Lack of electrical and phone outlets in general, and on decks and porches in particular.

Interior Flow

When you examine a house's interior, you'll be considering every room, of course, but you'll also want to think long and hard about traffic patterns and traffic flow and about the juxtaposition of the various rooms. See if you can tell whether the architect really thought about how people would live their daily lives in the house.

For example, you come home with your minivan stuffed with groceries. How easy will it be to unload? Or it's your turn to host Thanksgiving dinner. Is the kitchen located conveniently close to the dining room? Or guests are coming for the weekend. Where will they sleep and which bathroom will they use?

The questions to ask are as varied as the events in your life and as mundane as the "daily grind." You should ask them of yourself with each house you see, if only because it is good practice. Once you find a house you're serious about, you should really bear down and devote some serious mental energy to this task.

If the house is empty, see if the real estate agent will give you the keys so you can go there alone. If not, arrange for another viewing, but this time take a tape measure, graph paper, and a camera to draw up an accurate floor plan. Once you're back home, sit with your floor plan and photographs and imagine living there.

As anyone who has seen *This Old House* on

television knows, there is nothing about a house that cannot be changed. Walls can be moved or eliminated, closets can be turned into bathrooms, the entire floor plan can be rearranged. But even if money is no object, redoing a house is always easier if it was thoughtfully designed in the first place.

Rooms and Activities

Once you've thought about how the house floor plan "works" (or doesn't work), you can zero in on specific rooms. Here again the key is to consider how you and your family will live in them. It really would not be a bad idea to make a list of all the things you do or may be doing in your daily life. You cook, you clean, you do laundry and iron the occasional shirt or blouse. You entertain friends, watch TV and videos, surf the Internet, and sleep. If children are in the picture, they'll need a safe place to play, a quiet place to do their homework, and a room where they can entertain friends once they become teenagers.

Obvious points? Of course. But easy to lose sight of when you're in the grip of house-buying fever. So take the time to make the list and expend the energy to imagine how you will do each of those things in the house. Then take a deep breath and admit to yourself that no house will be perfect.

Even if you build your own house, you'll have to make trade-offs and compromises. The key point is to become aware of as many layout and design imperfections as possible before you buy. You don't want to come home to your new hillside

F.Y.I.

According to the *Wall Street Journal,* one in every eight U.S. households today has at least one adult working full-time from home, either as a self-employed person or a telecommuter. That number is expected to rise to one in every five (20 percent) households by 2002 as a result of a tight labor market, the ever-expanding reach of computer networks, and a growing appreciation for home and personal values versus workplace necessities. That means a four-bedroom home may be easier to sell in years to come, since many buyers will turn at least one bedroom into an office.

split-level with your first load of groceries and only then realize that from now on, you'll be carrying them up two flights of stairs to the kitchen. You may buy the house anyway, but at least you'll go in with your eyes open.

Kitchens

The kitchen is the heart of every home. Even if the schedules of your family members make it difficult to sit down to dinner at the same time, the kitchen is still where the food is—and the microwave, dishwasher, oven, and stove. So, whether you're doing a little recreational cooking with your significant other, making a meal for company, or trying to get something on the table quickly for your Little Leaguer at six and your high school drama star after rehearsals at eight, the way the kitchen "works" is crucial.

Do you have enough countertop space for your electric mixer, toaster oven, coffee grinder, and food processor? Is the dishwasher located next to the sink so you can easily scrape and load your dishes? Where will you store your recyclables until trash day? Is there room for two of you to cook at the same time?

Bathrooms and Bedrooms

These days, one and a half bathrooms—which is to say a full bathroom near the bedrooms and a powder room near the living area—is pretty much the minimum. Indeed, the trend in newer homes in recent years has been toward "master suites" that are larger than many apartments, with big beds, big closets, and huge bathrooms sporting double sinks, a shower, a soaking tub or Jacuzzi, and room for a StairMaster or NordicTrack home gym. The kids may share a bathroom down the hall, and there may be a third full bath for the guest room, plus at least one powder room on the first floor.

Basically, the more bathrooms, the better, though you will want to stop to think about who will use each one and how. Is there enough room for you and your mate to get ready for work at the same time? Can your kids use their bathroom to get ready for school simultaneously? Is there shelf space to store cosmetics and supplies? Can you run two hair dryers at the same time without blowing a fuse?

Though you may not be able to afford it in a starter house, the ideal in many parts of the country is four bedrooms and two and a half bathrooms. Even if your family is small and you don't need so many rooms for sleeping, the extra space won't go to waste. Any extra rooms can become guest rooms, home offices, storage areas for off-season clothes, hobby rooms, libraries, and so on.

Speaking of storage, one thing you'll want to zero in on when considering bedrooms of any sort is closet space. Are the closets large enough for your clothes and shoes? Could they be enhanced by adding a shelf or a closet organizer? Would an armoire or free-standing wardrobe work in the room if the closets are too small?

Living Rooms

For literally thousands of years, homes have had rooms for daily living and rooms for entertaining visitors. The "drawing rooms" of English novels, for example, had nothing to do with art. The term was short for "withdrawing" and referred to the custom of the ladies leaving the men to their port and cigars in the formal dining room while they withdrew for conversation among themselves, to be rejoined later by the men, of course.

Similarly, the term "parlor" is derived from the French word for "speak." Not too long ago in America, the front parlor was where you entertained your guests and pastor while the back parlor was where you could take your shoes off, literally let your hair down, and put your feet up by the fire to read the paper or the latest installment by that popular new novelist Charles Dickens.

Today we call our entertaining rooms "living rooms," though not much living actually goes on there. Nor does much entertaining. In these days of informality, you are more likely to have your guests in the kitchen chopping vegetables as you prepare to serve dinner on the deck, patio, or porch.

So perhaps the living room won't really be very important. Can it be used for something else? Could the space be turned into an office of some sort? A downstairs bedroom? These are questions you need to ask.

Family Rooms

You are likely to use the family room, our modern term for "back parlor," almost as much as your kitchen. You may also hear the terms "recreation room," "rec room," "den," or "media room." But to cut to the chase, where will the family watch TV?

In many households, the ideal is to have the kitchen not only close to the family room, but almost a part of it. That way, the person who is cooking or cleaning up or serving dinner or dessert will not be cut off from the group. The others won't have to stop the video that has been rented, for example. The person in the kitchen can continue to monitor (and comment upon) what's on the TV.

Home Inspections

You can rely on your own instincts to evaluate the overall design and livability of a house, but once you get serious about a property, you should have the place gone over by a licensed home inspector. Typically, the written offer you make on the house will be subject to having the house inspected. You may also want to include separate stipulations regarding termite infestations and radon. If the house gets its drinking water from a well, it is also a good idea to have the water tested for coliform bacteria.

The inspector will prepare a report for you, but if at all possible, schedule the inspection at a time when you can accompany the inspector and take detailed notes. The inspector will examine and test furnaces, air conditioners, gas and electrical services, and other "systems," as well as any appliances that will be left in the house.

Inspectors will estimate the age of an appliance and tell how much longer it is likely to last. They'll see if the house has settled excessively for its age. They'll examine the roof for leaks and suggest ways to improve the energy efficiency of the house. In most instances, they will also tell you what a given repair, improvement, or replacement is likely to cost. That's important, because any serious problem de-

SMART MONEY

Nationally syndicated real estate columnist David W. Myers points out that "the inspector's job is to tell you about the home's current shortcomings and alert you to problems that may develop in the future. It's important to realize that most home inspectors are generalists, not specialists. They know a lot about the general components of a home and can usually identify problem areas. But few inspectors are qualified to make specific recommendations about needed repairs."

So should your inspector identify a truly serious problem—like a leaking roof—you should follow up by hiring a licensed contractor who specializes in such problems to give you an estimate of what the repair would cost.

Improvements That Add Value

Which improvements add the greatest value to a home? According to *Remodeling* magazine, a publication of the National Association of Home Builders, remodeling the kitchen returns the most. Here's what you can expect for some of the most common home improvements. For more details, visit the National Association of Home Builders Web site (www.nahb.com/most.html).

Improvement	Cost of Job	Amount Recouped
Minor kitchen remodel	$8,395	102%
Bathroom addition	$11,721	92%
Major kitchen remodel	$22,509	90%
Master suite	$37,388	87%
Family room addition	$32,558	86%
Home office conversion	$8,179	69%
Replace windows	$5,976	68%

manding immediate attention will become a factor in your negotiations with the seller.

Indeed, there is a growing demand for home inspections. After all, a home is the largest single investment for most purchasing families, and as we saw in chapter 2, repair costs over a period of thirty years can amount to four times what you paid for the house. (It's at the ten-year mark that repair and maintenance costs typically kick in with urgency and force, and, of course, they continue from there on as one thing after another has to be fixed, remodeled, or replaced.) In addition, people do have a tendency to sue each other these days, so there has been increased concern about full disclosure in home-buying transactions.

The American Society of Home Inspectors (www.ashi.com) and the National Association of Home Inspectors (www.nahi.org) are the leading professional organizations in this area. And, by the way, laymen will find the ASHI site on the World Wide Web quite informative. The site's library section, for example, includes articles and links related to topics like "Chimneys and Flues," "Aluminum Wiring," "Buried Oil Tanks," and "Choosing a Roofing Contractor."

It is important to note, however, that architects may also do home inspecting. "I could tell you some real horror stories," says Steve Harberts, an architect and member of the American Institute of Architects (www.aiaonline.com). "Some of the worst problems [in California] were in hillside homes. In some cases, there were gross building code violations, or no permits for major additions added to homes."

Harberts, who has been a practicing architect for nearly thirty years, usually charges a flat fee of $250 for a home inspection. "Generally I base my fee on one hundred dollars per hour, and a typical inspection takes about two and a half hours." He notes that home inspections will not provide a warranty or guarantee that the property is trouble-free. Nor will it assure you that the home currently complies with all local codes.

But, according to the National Association of Home Inspectors (NAHI), it definitely reduces the amount of risk involved because it alerts you to problems you might not even think to look for. Any home involved in a transaction can benefit from an inspection. But homes older than ten years are most likely to *need* an inspection.

SMART SOURCES

When choosing a home inspector, insist on one who is a member—not just someone who "follows the standards"—of the American Society of Home Inspectors (ASHI). For a list of members in your area, call ASHI at 800-743-2744. You may also want to ask to see a typical report to get an idea of the inspector's thoroughness and the amount of detail reported.

The Most Common Problems

According to a member survey conducted by the American Society of Home Inspectors, the nine problems inspectors encounter most frequently are:

1. Improper surface grading and drainage, which can lead to water in the basement.

2. Improper or inadequate electrical wiring.

3. Roof damage.

4. Blocked chimneys and other heating system problems.

5. Cracked or peeling paint, crumbling masonry, makeshift wiring or plumbing, and generally poor overall maintenance.

6. Structural problems with foundation walls, floor joists, and rafters.

7. Plumbing defects.

8. Sloppy caulking around windows and similar exterior workmanship flaws.

9. Poor ventilation, which can lead to excessive interior moisture and, eventually, to wood rot.

The Fixer-Upper

There are times when buying a home in obvious need of updating and repair can actually be a good thing. A home can fall into disrepair for any number of reasons. Perhaps the current owners are elderly and living on a fixed income. Or the owners may be separated or in the midst of a divorce. As long as the location is good, buying such a dwelling could be a bargain.

If this is the case, you will want to take extra care to be more thorough than ever in your inspections. And when you finally do own the property, you'll have to think carefully about the improvements you make. If your goal is to resell the house at a fat profit a few years from now, you may spend less on each improvement than if you plan to stay there yourself for the long-term.

Of course, whether you buy a fixer-upper, a starter house, or a brand-new "executive" home in a fashionable development, it will at long last be yours. And as the moving van pulls away, you can finally give into your emotions, look around, and say, with feeling, "There's no place like home!"

THE BOTTOM LINE

You can change anything in a house for a price, but it is much better to begin with a well-designed structure. Ignore just about everything you hear from the real estate agent or from the owners. If they mislead you or claim, say, that the roof doesn't leak when they know that it does, you can always take them to court. But that's expensive. It's far better to spend the $300 or so needed to hire a home inspector. Basically, assume that regardless of what the law says, you are in a "let the buyer beware" situation.

Do not let emotions take control. Do not hear what you want to hear and let yourself convert opinions or vague statements into genuine facts. As the potential buyer you are very much in the driver's seat.

CHAPTER 7

Offers and Negotia- tions

• The more you know about the sellers of a property—why they're selling, where they're going, their feelings about the house—the better.

• Real estate negotiations are about more than just price. Closing dates, occupancy dates, personal property left in the house, and many other elements may come into play.

• Before making your offer, study comparable sales in the last six months to get an idea of the price range. Then offer at the low end of that range.

• Don't give the seller any more than forty-eight hours to accept or reject your offer or to make a counteroffer.

• Improve your offer's chances of acceptance by getting preapproved for a mortgage loan of the necessary amount.

Well, here you are. You've decided at last that you really want to own your own home, town house, co-op, or condo. You've calculated how much you can comfortably afford. You've done your research and have identified one or more desirable locations. You've found a buyer's agent or a traditional real estate agent whom you like. And you've found a property. You love the place and can easily see yourself and your family living there for years to come. It is just what you've always wanted. Now what?

Now's the time for an emotional cold shower. Let your feelings run their course, but stay above them. When you have finished imagining what life would be like living there, admit to yourself that you could be equally happy living someplace else. Once again, there is no one "perfect" place for you to live. No single property will ever completely fulfill your mental ideal.

But there are a lot of properties that come very close. So relax. It's not only good for your blood pressure but good for your pocketbook. That's because if you fail to play it cool, you could easily end up paying thousands of dollars more for your dream house than necessary.

Mortgages and finances are covered in the next chapter. The focus here is on the process of negotiating the sale price.

Know Your Opponent

"Know the enemy. Know yourself. And you can fight a hundred battles with no danger of defeat," wrote Sun Tzu in the early fourth-century classic

The Art of War. Niccolò Machiavelli offered much the same advice in *The Prince* in 1513. Today we would say, "Try to get inside your opponent's head. Find out what they want and use this knowledge to get what you want."

The people who are selling the house you want to buy may be very nice people. They may even be just like you. Indeed, they probably *are* just like you. After all, you're both attracted to the same house. They are not your enemy. But they are your opponents, for their interests (getting the most money for the house) are the exact opposite of yours (paying as little as possible).

The less the sellers know about the pressures or constraints you may be under and the more you know about them, the better you are likely to do. Why are they selling? Where are they going? What kind of people are they? Are they emotionally attached to the home or eager to leave? What hints can you pick up as you walk through the house?

Traditional real estate agents will do everything possible to keep you away from the sellers. They want to avoid the possibility of personality conflicts souring the deal. And they don't want to take a chance on the sellers giving away an important piece of information, such as the date one of them has to start a new job out of state.

If you're using a buyer's broker, on the other hand, meeting the sellers should not be a problem, should you want to do so. Be aware, however, that such a meeting can cut both ways. The sellers may not like you or the idea of your living in "their" house. Your best bet is likely to be to use your buyer's broker to find out everything you can.

A Little "Game Theory"

Trust the "market" and you can't go too far wrong. But you must make the effort to discover what the market says. Therefore, you should politely ignore your real estate agent when he or she says, "They're asking 180, but I think they would take 165." Don't let the agent set the range of the price negotiation. Instead say, "That's interesting, but comparable properties have been selling in the high 150s. Suppose we offered 158?"

This is the game-playing part of the process, which some buyers love and others absolutely hate. And it's gaming as in "game theory," the applied mathematics presented by von Neumann and Morgenstern in their 1944 title, *The Theory of Games and Economic Behavior.* What cards do the sellers hold? What are their hot buttons? What are your hot buttons and weaknesses? How can each of you "play" to make the best possible deal, given what each of you knows about the other?

No need to get too cerebral here. Just be aware that however much you may want to buy, the current owners may want to sell even more. They may have accepted a job transfer to another state and are under pressure from the boss to move quickly. They may be concerned about getting settled and getting the kids into school in time. Or the sellers may be under no pressure at all, in which case they'll be perfectly content to wait things out until the market rises to meet their price. Uncertainty is the essence of game theory, so the more you know about your opponents and their needs—and the less your opponents know about you—the stronger your negotiating position.

The Elements of a Deal

The first thing to remember—after you remember to put your emotions away and operate with nothing but cool intellect—is that price isn't everything. A seller may be asking a certain price but be willing to take $10,000 less if you can complete the transaction in three weeks. Why? Because the sellers may be under pressure from an employer to move to a new location, or under the gun on a deal to buy their own new house in a different neighborhood.

Similarly, the sellers may be willing to accept less if you'll agree to complete the transaction but delay taking possession for a month, during which you would rent the house to them while they get their affairs in order. Or you may say, "We want to move in August First," and the sellers may respond with "How about September First, and we'll reduce the price by $5,000?"

Of course, it can work the opposite way too. In a "seller's market," where there aren't enough desirable houses to satisfy demand, sellers can name their own terms. They can say, "This is my price. It is nonnegotiable. And, by the way, if you want the house, you will be paying my real estate agent's commission as well."

Negotiating Points

Every person, property, and situation is unique, but all home-buying transactions involve certain standard details. Each of these can be a point for

According to Dr. Gary Eldred, executive director of the National Initiative for Home Ownership, the three main negotiating styles of buyers are passive-accommodating, adversarial, and win-win. Too much money is involved to be passive, no matter how much you hate confrontation. And it is stupid to squeeze every last concession out of a seller. You need the seller's goodwill, for until you move in, they still occupy "your" house.

Win-win negotiators, in contrast, "primarily work to secure a strong, mutually beneficial agreement that everyone is committed to seeing to completion." Everyone walks away satisfied, in other words.

SMART DEFINITION

Fixture

An article that was once personal property but has been so affixed to real estate that it has become real property (such as stoves, carpeting, bookcases, and plumbing). Generally, the test of whether or not an item is a fixture depends more on the firmness of its installation than on the size of the hole that might be caused by its removal.

negotiation as part of the larger deal. It all depends on how important each point is to you and to the seller.

• **Closing date.** The date when the final papers will be signed and the checks will be written. A seller buying another house will want to close as soon as possible, but you'll need time to secure your financing and handle other details.

• **Occupancy date.** The date by which the sellers will have vacated the property. If you currently live in an apartment, you will want to move in as soon as possible to avoid paying any more rent than necessary. Ideally the sellers should be out before the closing. (Sad to say, there have been cases in which the former owners have refused to leave, even after they have sold the house.) If not, they should pay you rent for any days they occupy the house after you've bought it.

• **Closing costs.** These include title insurance, pro-rated real estate taxes, pro-rated mortgage interest, attorney's fees, the surveyor's fee, the pest inspection fee, the fee for recording the deed, and possibly a real estate transfer tax. Closing costs can total 3 to 6 percent of the mortgage amount, or 2 to 5 percent of the purchase price.

If you are unable to qualify for a loan large enough to cover these costs, the seller might be willing to split some of them with you or even pay them completely to make the deal go through.

• **Fixtures and personal property.** In most states, unless they have been specifically excluded by the seller, items that have been literally "affixed" to the property are considered part of the property. Switch plates, ceiling fans, chandeliers, wall sconces, built-in bookcases, curtain rods and blinds, and wall-to-wall carpet are good examples of fixtures. But what about the drapes? What about the new SubZero refrigerator? The window air conditioner? Do not assume *anything*. Part of the deal should be determining which items of personal property stay with the house, and spelling it out in writing.

"Magic Money"

The late Senator Everett Dirksen is credited with saying, "A billion here, a billion there—and pretty soon you're talking about real money." The senator was referring to the disconnect between the money the government spends and the real world.

Something similar happens when the average person buys or sells a house. Most people focus on the monthly payment, for that's something they can feel. But people who would never in their lives write out a check for $10,000 for anything often find themselves dealing with such amounts as casually as if they were playing poker with fifty-cent chips in a local bar.

That's because the money doesn't seem real. It's "magic money," and it works both ways. The sellers figure their house has appreciated $50,000 since they bought it. If they have to sell the property for $5,000 to $10,000 less than they had hoped for, they're still tens of thousands of dollars ahead. It's not as though someone had put that $50,000 in their hands and they are now required to peel off five of their fifty one-thousand-dollar bills. It's magic money. Similarly, if you must pay five or ten thousand more than you wanted to pay to get a property, you'll say, "Well, it only adds a couple of

SMART SOURCES

Real estate sales are a matter of public record. To find out what the current owners paid for their house, check with the Recorder of Deeds or your local equivalent at your county courthouse. Note that some counties now make this information available online. You might also check KnowX ("Your Courthouse on the Web") at www.knowx.com. You can search by name or by address. Each report costs $6.95.

bucks to our monthly mortgage payment. And besides, we'll be moving in five years anyhow."

How Much to Offer

"Magic money" is an important concept. It exists because when you buy or sell real estate, you are playing your part in the rough-and-tumble edge of a market economy. Most sellers will test the market. They will look at what comparable homes have sold for recently and price their property just a bit higher. They will expect to negotiate. Buyers also expect to negotiate, so they will offer to pay something lower than the asking price. Tens of thousands of dollars may be involved, but it's all magic money until a deal is struck.

So how do you decide how much to offer? There are no rules, but here is an excellent general guideline: Try to determine the fair market value of the house by looking at the range within which comparable homes have sold in the last six months. Then offer a price at the low end of that range. Your real estate professional will be able to show you the "comps" (as they are called) and to advise you on how much to offer. Once again, remember that if yours is a traditional agent, he or she is motivated to get the sellers as much as possible for the home.

Potential Pitfalls

You are under no obligation to offer the figure your real estate professional suggests, but you should certainly give it strong consideration. That's because the market is the most important factor in determining what you will end up paying, and real estate pros know the market. The comps they show you should serve as good evidence of the fair-market-value range of the house.

Still, it is very important to pay close attention, for after they have been lived in, no two houses are ever precisely comparable. Indeed, even two identical brand-new houses in a development may not be absolutely comparable. One may have a nicer view, a backyard that borders on a park, or if it's a condo unit, one might be closer to the pool (which could be a plus or a minus).

Estimating fair market value is anything but an exact science. For example, you may be interested in a center-hall colonial, but one of the comps that sold recently is a ranch-style house, so your real estate professional will have to make adjustments for square footage, lot size, amenities, and so on. Or your house may be located in an older neighborhood in which each house is unique and therefore very difficult to compare.

If you've lived in an area for a while and have paid attention to the real estate ads in the newspapers, you yourself will begin to develop a sense of the market. But if you're moving in from out of town, particularly if you're moving from an area where housing costs are relatively high to one where they are relatively low, even the seller's asking price may seem low. To avoid overpaying, be sure to look at the comps.

You should also be aware that, while sellers and buyers normally expect to negotiate to arrive at a price between "asked" and "offered," the market sometimes surprises them both. It is not at all uncommon in some areas for a seller to receive several nearly simultaneous offers, some of which may actually be higher than the asking price. That probably means that the asking price was set too low, but who knew? In such situations, if you offer less than the asking price, the sellers probably won't respond to your offer at all. Once again, you should listen to the advice of a seasoned professional.

Finally, you should probably resist the urge to "low-ball"—to make an initial offer far below what the sellers would assume someone would offer. You may think you're being really sharp by adjusting the seller's expectations downward. If the house has been on the market for several months, you may think this gives you an advantage. But that could be a miscalculation. The sellers might take your low-ball offer as a personal insult, for to them it says, "I think you're so desperate to sell that I can take advantage of you and steal this house by paying a price far below its fair market value."

The Formal Process

Nothing means anything in a real estate deal until it is written down and signed off on by both parties. For the sake of speed and convenience, buyer and seller can converse with each other through their agents regarding the details—the price, personal property, the closing date, and so on. But at some point, usually sooner rather than later, a formal written offer must be submitted to the seller.

The form that written offer takes depends on where you live and is generally controlled by custom, not by law. In some areas, it is common to prepare a one-page offer form with a clause stating that the offer is subject to the signing of a mutually acceptable purchase contract within a certain number of days.

While it seems clean and simple, this approach is not in the buyer's best interests. That's because the offer document is not legally binding. The danger is that someone else will jump in and top your offer before the actual purchase contract is signed.

Elsewhere, the offer takes the form of an actual real estate purchase contract (REPC) that specifies all the details of the proposed deal. In such cases, it is very important to realize that, if accepted by the seller, this contract *is* the deal. It becomes a legally binding contract.

Local and state realtor boards and government agencies provide general forms, but you should be aware that there is no such thing as a "standard" purchase contract in this country. So while you may want to use the preprepared forms as a starting point, you are free to modify or remove any terms you disagree with and add clauses you want to have included.

SMART MONEY

According to syndicated real estate columnist David W. Myers, "Buyers should always include a clause in their purchase offer that gives the seller only twenty-four to forty-eight hours to either accept the offer or make a counteroffer." Giving the seller any more leeway "provides ample time for the seller's agent to show your offer to competing buyers and secure a higher bid."

Items in the Contract

The REPC and offer forms used by your real estate professional are designed to cover all the major points and contingencies. There will be blanks and language for how long your offer stands, your down-payment amount, how real estate taxes will be paid, the title insurance company that will be used, the date you will all meet to close the deal, the date by which the sellers will vacate the property, the right to a final walk-through prior to the closing, the house inspection contingency, and more.

Jane, 47, is an advertising agency account executive. The house she and her husband wanted had been on the market for a month, and there had been no offers. "The sellers were divorced and living in different states," Jane recalls. "The contract had to be signed by each of them, so we felt we had to give them five business days. Our agent FedExed the offer on Monday. On Thursday she called and said, 'There's been another offer. It's ten thousand dollars more than yours.' We were devastated. There was simply no way we could match it, so we lost the house. We're still looking. But when we make our next offer, we'll give the sellers no more than forty-eight hours to respond!"

Ideally, you would have an attorney review the agreement before signing it. A preprinted form approved by the state board of realtors may or may not be a good agreement, but at least the language cannot be changed without crossing something out. This is not the case with a form generated by a real estate agent's computer. If there isn't time for an attorney review, at least make sure that you either fill out or put a line or an "N/A" for "Not Applicable" in any blank that someone else could fill in to change the terms after you've signed the agreement.

Special Points

Your real estate professional will be able to advise you on most details of the offer or contract. But several points bear special consideration. First, don't give the sellers more than twenty-four to forty-eight hours to accept your offer or make a counteroffer. That makes it too easy for the seller's agent to contact others who may have expressed an interest in the property and say, "I have a firm offer of $145,000. If you folks want this property, you'd better make your offer immediately."

Second, you'll have to put up thousands of dollars long before you go to settlement, so be prepared. Typically, your offer will be accompanied by "binder" or "earnest" money. This is usually $500 to $1,000, though in some parts of the country, the amount may be 1 to 3 percent of the purchase price. The purpose of this money is to show the seller that you are serious.

Several days after your offer is accepted you will probably also have to make a deposit payment equal to as much as 10 percent of the sale price. This not only shows you're serious, it is serious money. Technically, if you default on the purchase, the seller can keep your deposit money as "liquidated damages." These damages may include the cost of the title search, possibly part of the agent's commission, and the loss of time and opportunity to sell the house to someone else. Not incidentally, it also makes it difficult for the average person to enter into another real estate contract with a different seller.

The handling and holding of earnest money and deposits may be a matter of law or a matter of local custom. In many states, the monies must be deposited into an interest-bearing escrow account and cannot be withdrawn until the "consummation or termination" of the agreement of sale. If at all possible, avoid situations in which the seller has direct control of the money. Should there be a disagreement causing you to withdraw from the deal, even if you are completely justified under the terms of the agreement, you may have to sue the seller to get your money back. And a lawsuit can cost you more than the deposit itself.

Finally, if you were the seller, which offer would you take, one that was a few thousand less than you had hoped to get but that is accompanied by a letter from a lender preapproving a mortgage of the required amount, or one that was a few thousand more that was contingent upon the buyer getting a loan at a certain interest rate? There are no simple answers, but the first offer is about as close as you're going to come to a "sure thing." Maybe the second buyer will be approved by his lender, but maybe not.

The point is that if you are going to play the house-buying game, you should give yourself every advantage over competing buyers. And from a seller's perspective, few things are more attractive

SMART DEFINITION

Contingency

A provision placed in a contract that requires the completion of a certain act or the happening of a particular event before that contract is binding. Typical contingencies include pulling out of the deal if you can't get the loan specified in the contract, or if you don't approve of the inspection report, or if you are unable to reach agreement with the seller on who will be responsible for any repairs.

THE BOTTOM LINE

Negotiating the price of a home is a complex, even scary process. Yet tens of thousands of people do it successfully every day, thanks in no small measure to the skills, experience, and knowledge of real estate professionals. Certainly there are exceptions, but in general, the powerful forces of supply and demand insure that most houses, condos, town houses, and co-ops sell for a "fair price." That means that the market will make sure that you won't get a property for much less than someone else would.

But the market offers no similar guard against overpaying. That's why you must pay attention. Look at the sales of comparable properties within the last six months. Keep your emotions in check and remember there is no single home that is right for you.

than an offer that is not overloaded with contingencies and that is made by someone who has been preapproved by a mortgage lender. And lenders and mortgages just happen to be the subject of the next chapter.

What You Need to Know about Mortgages

Money—It's Just Another "Product"

Although you may consider appearing before the Almighty to account for your life would be preferable to pleading your case before a loan officer, nothing could be further from the truth. There is nothing magical about a mortgage. It's just money, and money is just another product. And as the borrower, you're the *customer*, not some groveling supplicant.

For example, if your credit record or work history are less than perfect, you may be charged a higher rate than someone else. But you are still the customer—the person whose payments, whose hard-earned dollars, are responsible for the lender's profits. And if lenders don't lend, they don't make any profits. So let's get real about who has the upper hand.

All you need to become a *confident* customer is an understanding of how the mortgage industry works. That is what this chapter will teach you. Then, in the following chapter, you'll learn how to roll up your sleeves and aggressively shop for the mortgage you want.

The Purity of Money

As a product, nothing is purer than money. A dollar is worth a dollar, regardless of whether it is crisp, clean, and new or crumpled, dirty, and torn. There is no question of excess mileage, physical location, or any of the other similar variables that figure into the purchase price or rental fees for all other products.

Obvious as it may seem, this fact has profound implications, particularly when it comes to home mortgages. First, because a dollar is always a dollar, financial markets can be very efficient. So if the Federal Reserve raises interest rates today, it's unlikely that you'll find some bank tomorrow that hasn't followed suit. It is not as though the money that one bank has to lend is in any better or worse condition than any other bank's funds.

In a broader sense, it means that if you want to borrow a certain amount of money, the cheapest loans you can find will end up costing you about the same regardless of how they are configured. One lender may give you a low rate but charge higher fees, while another may offer a slightly higher rate and no fees.

You've got to shop. After all, lenders will happily charge an uninformed customer as much as they can. That's business. But when you do shop, you will discover that almost everyone is using the same playbook. Thus, given your income, net worth, and the property you want to buy, you are going to pay pretty much the same, regardless of the lender you choose.

It's All about Risk

Not everyone pays the same price to borrow the same amount of money. The price you'll pay begins with the price lenders must pay for the money themselves. In the simplest terms, this would be the interest rate a bank pays on the money people have deposited in savings accounts. A percentage for profit is added, of course, but the main pricing element is *risk*. The greater the risk the bank perceives, the more you will have to pay to borrow the money. That's why:

• Fixed-rate 30-year mortgages cost more than 15-year mortgages. (Should interest rates rise, the bank would not want to be locked into a long loan at a low rate.)

• Jumbos—loans over the Fannie Mae maximum of $227,150 for 1998—cost more than loans less than the Fannie Mae limit. (A greater sum of money is at risk.)

• The lower the down payment, the higher the interest rate. (The less money the buyers put down up front, the less there is for them to lose if they later default and walk away from the loan and the property.)

• Your credit rating, total debt, length of time at your current residence, employment history, years of formal schooling, and retirement account and other assets are carefully considered by the lender. (Statistically, someone who isn't "steady" is a greater risk than someone who settles down.)

Everything Is Negotiable!

Risk assessment is not an exact science. So if you're on the margin—say, with a credit history that is almost but not quite perfect—one lender may be willing to give you a better interest rate and more favorable terms than another. That's when it really pays to shop around.

Also, one of the ways lenders boost their profit is by charging various fees. These fees are often negotiable, as is the commission the loan originator earns on the deal. Much depends on the strength of your financial situation and on how badly the lender wants your business. But for the time being, you should begin your mortgage quest assuming that absolutely everything is negotiable.

The Art of the Deal: Principal, Interest Rate, Points, and Term

As noted earlier, there is nothing magical about a mortgage. It is simply an agreement between you and the lender regarding the following elements:

• Principal (the amount of money you're borrowing)

• Interest rate (the fee you agree to pay for "renting" the money, expressed as a percentage of the borrowed amount)

• Points (part of the interest paid in advance in return for a lower interest rate for the life of the loan)

• Term (the length of time over which you agree to pay the interest and repay the principal)

These four components are the main parts of every mortgage, but they can be configured many different ways. For example, you may be able to pay an up-front fee of, say, 1 or more percent of

F.Y.I.

In October 1998, the Census Bureau reported that the median length of time adults lived in their homes was 5.2 years. That means that half of the adult population lived in their home for less than 5.2 years, and that half lived in their homes for a longer period of time. Renters stayed in one residence for a median of 2.1 years, compared with 8.2 years for people living in apartments and condos that they owned.

The Census Bureau report "Seasonality of Moves and Duration of Residence, P70-66" also said that although 16.7 percent of the population moved in 1993, nearly 15.3 percent lived in the same house for more than twenty years.

the loan amount—in mortgage-speak, 1 percent is one *point*—and an interest rate of 6.75 percent. Or the same lender may offer you a rate of 7.25 percent and no points. (The term "discount points" refers to the same thing.) If you keep this concept in mind, shopping for a mortgage will be much less confusing.

What Does Your Future Hold?

Mortgages are not only about risk. They are also about the future, a fact that is important to remember in the midst of your current excitement over buying a house. Thus, if you take out a 30-year loan, the details of the loan are configured on the assumption that you will stay in the house for the next thirty years.

Of course, no one expects you to *actually* do this. More than likely, you'll move to another house long before the mortgage has been paid off. This has always been the case. But years ago, the length of time you planned to stay in a house didn't matter because most lenders offered little more than a plain 30-year mortgage. Today there are lots of other mortgage options, many of which offer significantly lower monthly payments in the early years of the term.

The Three Major Types of Mortgages

The three main types of mortgages available today are *fixed-rate*, *adjustable-rate*, and *balloon*. As the term implies, the interest rate on a fixed-rate mortgage stays the same for the life of the loan. That's the traditional way of doing things. With adjustable-rate mortgages (ARMs), the rate you're charged varies with the money markets. Balloon mortgages offer generally low, fixed-rate payments for several years, after which the entire balance of the loan is due in one large "balloon payment."

Naturally, there are variations on these major themes. But don't think of them as complications, think of them as options that make it easier to find a deal that best suits your needs. And don't forget, if those needs (or interest rates) change in the future, you can almost certainly *refinance* and replace your current mortgage with a different deal. Here's a rundown of the kinds of mortgages you'll encounter:

• **Fixed-rate.** You pay the same interest rate for the life of the loan, usually fifteen or thirty years. The two main advantages are the certainty that your monthly payment will never increase and the possibility of locking in a low interest rate when you think rates may be on the rise. It is precisely because of this risk that lenders typically charge a bit higher rate than they do for ARMs.

• **Fixed-adjustable hybrids.** You get a fixed rate for three, five, seven, or ten years, after which the loan is converted to an adjustable rate. The fixed rate tends to be higher than that of an ARM but less than that of a pure fixed-rate mortgage. This means lower monthly payments during the fixed-rate part of the term, which should make a given house more affordable. Chances are, by the time the loan converts to an adjustable rate, you'll be making more money, so a possibly higher monthly payment won't throw you. Such loans are also called *intermediate ARMs.*

• **Two-step fixed-rate loans.** With this thirty-year product you are charged a rate that is usually lower than the current fixed-rate percentage for the first seven years. Then you are charged a rate that is slightly higher than the rate current at that

Eight Questions to Ask about an ARM

Longtime *Newsweek* columnist and financial expert Jane Bryant Quinn suggests that anyone shopping for an adjustable-rate mortgage ask the following questions:

1. *What is the ARM's interest rate linked to?* The six-month or one-year Treasury bill rates are often used. And, because American mortgages are popular with European investors, the Eurodollar-based London Inter-bank Offer Rate (LIBOR) is also used. The Cost of Funds rate index (COFi) of the Federal Home Loan Bank board's 11th District (California, Arizona, and Nevada) is another frequently used ARM index. The Cost of Funds rate tends to lag behind other indexes, a good thing when rates are generally rising, but not so good when rates are falling. Quinn says, "Over a whole interest-rate cycle, a mortgage linked to short-term Treasuries should cost less and is the easiest to follow in the newspapers."

2. *What is the ARM's margin?* Be sure to find out how many points the lender adds to the benchmark index to come up with the rate you will be charged. If two lenders use the same index but add different markups, go with the lender using the smaller markup.

3. *What is the teaser rate and how long does it apply?* The teaser rate is usually one to three points lower than the loan's regular rate. Typically it lasts only one to three years.

4. *How often is the interest rate and payment amount adjusted?* Some ARMs adjust every year, some adjust every six months. When rates are falling, frequent adjustments are good for you. When they are rising, frequent adjustments are bad. The reason for asking this question is to get a sense of what you can expect to pay each year.

time for the remaining twenty-three years. Normally, the lender agrees that this second rate will not be any more than five or six points higher than the rate you had at the beginning of the loan. Such loans are also called *7/23s.*

• **Adjustable-rate mortgage (ARM).** Lenders typically charge a *margin* (or markup) of one to three

5. *What are the caps?* ARMs have annual caps and overall caps. The annual cap limits the number of points your rate can rise in any year or adjustment. The overall cap is a ceiling limiting the maximum rate you will pay, regardless of what happens to interest rates. Choose the loan with the lower caps.

6. *Is there an interest-rate floor?* Some lenders will limit how low your interest rate can go. Good for the lender, not so good for you. Try for an ARM that does not have a floor.

7. *Can the loan be converted to a fixed-rate mortgage in the future?* This option can save you from paying points and closing costs should you want to convert the loan. But lenders typically charge extra for ARMs with this feature. There may be a higher up-front fee or a slightly higher interest rate for your ARM. Since no one can predict where interest rates will go, and since you can almost always refinance a mortgage, you will probably be better off not paying for this feature.

8. *Is the loan guaranteed?* Be sure to ask your prospective lender what happens if interest rates shoot up above the loan's lifetime cap. Can the lender force you to refinance and accept a different deal? Will you be required to pass a credit check for the new loan? Look at the fine print. See if there are any loopholes permitting the lender to change the terms of the deal.

Jane Bryant Quinn also advises anyone with an ARM to keep an eye out to see if the loan continues to be competitive. "These loans are cheap in the early years, but in later years the lenders may charge slightly more than the going interest rate. Consider refinancing with a new ARM if you can get a low teaser rate and the new loan doesn't raise your lifetime cap."

points over some official benchmark *index rate*, like the current One-Year Treasury Constant Maturity rate. Rates are usually adjusted once or twice a year, but most ARM agreements stipulate an *annual cap* limiting the number of points the rate can be increased in any given year. The typical annual cap is about two points. Most agreements also include an *overall cap* that limits the total number of percentage points your rate can be increased over the life of the loan. At this writing, an overall cap of six points is common.

Lenders typically use artificially low *teaser rates* to attract ARM borrowers. The teaser rate may actually be lower than the current benchmark, and it is often two to three points lower than that of a fixed-rate loan. But teaser rates last for only a limited period of time, usually one to three years.

• **Negative amortization ARMs.** These loans are bad news. Your monthly payment is fixed, but the interest rate that you are charged varies with the benchmark. If rates go up and your fixed payment is not large enough to cover the increase, the extra interest you owe is "added to your bill." It becomes part of the principal, and you begin paying interest on the interest. Fortunately, however, consumers have caught on, and "negative am" or "negative equity" loans have largely disappeared from the market.

• **Balloon mortgages.** This kind of mortgage charges you a low, fixed rate for five to seven years. At the end of that term, you will owe the balance of the loan in a single large payment. If you're certain that you will be selling your house before that balloon payment is due—because of an anticipated job transfer, for example—this type of mortgage may make good sense. Otherwise, you may find yourself being forced to accept whatever refinancing option a lender decides upon when the balloon payment comes due.

Why ARMs Are Likely to Be the Cheapest Option

Human beings like certainty. That's why fixed-rate mortgages have always been so popular. Unfortunately, certainty of this sort costs money. Fearful that interest rates may rise significantly over the 30-year term of a fixed-rate loan, lenders compensate by charging you a higher rate than they would if they did not have this risk. With an ARM, in contrast, that risk is greatly reduced, so they can charge you less.

The downside for you is that your interest rate can increase by as much as two points each year until the ARM's overall cap is reached. Your monthly payments may thus go up. But interest rates run in cycles—if they go up, they won't stay up for more than a few years. Eventually interest rates, and your monthly payment, will come down. Thus, over the course of the loan, an adjustable-rate mortgage will probably be your cheapest alternative.

Certainly you should calculate the worst-case scenario. What would your monthly payments be if the rate rises the maximum amount each year after the expiration of your teaser rate? What would they be if the overall cap rate were applied? Answering these questions will serve as a good

F.Y.I.

"Invest in inflation," said Will Rogers, "it's the only thing going up." Interest rates vary over time. But, historically, they are always pegged to the rate of inflation. That's why economists and investors distinguish between the "nominal interest rate"—the rate you are charged—and the "real interest rate"—the rate the lender actually earns.

The real interest rate is the nominal rate, minus the expected rate of inflation. Lenders know that you will be paying them back in years to come with dollars that are worth less than they are today, due to inflation. So they build their inflation expectations into the nominal rate they charge.

reality check, but this is only a small part of the equation.

Presumably your income will also rise over time. And some ARMs offer you the right to convert to a fixed-rate mortgage at some time in the future without paying closing costs again. (Lenders may charge you an extra upfront fee or raise your interest rate by a fraction of a percent if you choose to go with this feature, however.) In addi-

Trust, but Verify!

Judy is a former flight attendant who now coordinates special events for a large hotel in northern Florida. "We bought our home with an ARM and were quite pleased with the rate. In fact, I'm not sure we could have afforded the house if the payments had been any higher. But we were nervous about the annual adjustments.

"At about the fifth or sixth year an adjustment came from the bank that seemed a bit high. So I looked into it. It turned out that the bank had used the wrong benchmark, and it had rounded the rate up instead of rounding it down as it was supposed to do. I was furious. But then my training in dealing with people took over. I was calm and polite. It took a few phone calls, but I got it straightened out.

"But I will *never* simply accept what the bank says our payment should be again. I don't think it's deliberate, but people do make mistakes. And those mistakes can cost my husband and me money!"

Financial publisher HSH Associates estimates that between 20 and 30 percent of ARM interest rate adjustments are incorrect. They can be in your favor or in the lender's favor, but they are wrong. For important information and a Rate Change Worksheet, visit the HSH Web site (www.hsh.com/pamphlets/ack.html).

You might also want to contact the American Homeowners Foundation (800-489-7776) and Loantech (800-888-6781, www.loantech.com). Both of these organizations will check the accuracy of your ARM rate for a fee or a commission on any refund that you're owed.

tion, refinancing at some point in the future is almost always an option.

Finally, you should know that, unlike fixed-rate loans, adjustable-rate mortgages are often *assumable.* This means that when you sell your house, the buyer can take over the loan, which can add up to a savings of thousands of dollars for the buyer, because there won't be any points and other loan-related fees to pay at the closing. At the very least, that can make your house easier to sell.

Shop for Your Mortgage First!

Since shopping for a loan at the same time you're shopping for a house can be quite a challenge, you might want to consider shopping for your mortgage first. This is not as radical an idea as you may think. Most lenders will be willing to *prequalify* you, and some will even go so far as to grant a *preapproval* on your loan.

The prequalification process starts with the lender looking at your income, net worth, and monthly expenses and liabilities. Numbers will be crunched and a letter will be issued by the lender saying that you qualify for a mortgage of a certain amount. Lenders will typically prequalify you free of charge.

The preapproval process, in contrast, is the same as applying for a mortgage, so you'll have to pay the usual fees. At the end of this process, the lender issues a letter committing to lend you a certain amount of money, subject to an appraisal of the property you eventually decide to buy.

Being prequalified is good. Being preapproved is better. The main downside to the latter is that the application fees you've paid will have to be paid again if you later choose a different lender. In either case, you'll have a very good idea of the price of the home you can buy, and you will be in a much stronger position when negotiating with its seller. The seller won't have to worry about having the house off the market for a month while you try to qualify for a loan. And since the financing process has already been started, you will probably be able to close on the house sooner than competing buyers.

Consider a Lock-In

If you opt for preapproval, it may make sense to ask the lender about a *lock-in*. Also known as a *rate lock* or *rate commitment*, this is a lender's promise to offer you the same deal that's available today for some specified time, regardless of what happens to interest rates or market conditions.

A lock-in is not the same as a loan commitment. The commitment letter guarantees the loan amount. The lock-in guarantees the terms. Lock-ins of thirty to sixty days are common. Their purpose is usually to hold your deal for you while your application is processed and you make arrangements to have the house inspected and perform other tasks prior to the closing.

Naturally, many variations exist. You may be able to lock in the complete deal, or lock in the rate while the points charged are allowed to float with market conditions. Or you may be able to let both the rate and the points float after you have applied but before making settlement, an option that might make some sense if you think rates will remain level or go down.

Be sure to get any lock-in agreement in writing. And don't forget to ask about any fees that may be charged and whether or not they will count toward your closing costs. Also ask if interest rates drop during the lock-in period, will you be able to take advantage of them?

Job One: Check Your Credit Report

When you apply for a mortgage, one of the very first things the lender will do is get a copy of your credit report. That's why one of the best things you can do *before* darkening a banker's door is to get a copy yourself. If you've made late payments in the past or have other problems, now's the time to work on cleaning things up.

Payments made from 30 to 180 days after their due date are usually considered delinquent, and a record of the delinquency will remain on your report for seven years from the date of the missed payment. The best way to deal with this situation is to make sure that all your accounts are current and that any past-due bills are paid. Then make sure you keep paying your bills on time.

If judgments or tax liens have been entered against you, pay them, even if you don't agree with them. You can litigate later. Few lenders will make loans to people who have not paid what appear to be legally valid obligations, regardless of who was right or wrong.

Even if your record is perfect, it is wise to check

your report for any errors. Make sure, for example, that any credit-card accounts you have closed show up as closed. This is important, because whether you use it or not, lenders pay close attention to your available credit. So if you've canceled that Visa card, make sure it shows up as canceled. If you've been divorced recently, make sure that your former spouse's accounts are not on your credit report. And so on.

Your Credit-Report Rights

The three leading credit bureaus—Equifax, Experian (formerly TRW), and Trans Union—create and maintain files on the credit histories of more than 190 million people in the United States who have a department store charge account, car loan, student loan, home mortgage, or Visa, Master-Card, or other credit cards. They also incorporate information drawn from public records, such as bankruptcies, foreclosures, tax liens, and court judgments.

If you find inaccuracies in your credit report, notify the credit bureau of the mistakes; the law now requires that the errors be corrected within thirty days of your doing so. And, once notified of an error, the bank or other business that supplied the incorrect information is required to correct its records so that the same error doesn't keep appearing on your credit report.

You have the right to provide credit bureaus with a one hundred–word statement explaining the circumstances that relate to specific information in your report. Examples might include late payments due to an illness, a divorce-related problem, or a product dispute with a manufacturer.

Credit-reporting companies are required by law to include such statements in your credit report.

Experian, Equifax, and Trans Union charge most consumers $8 for a copy of a credit report, but if you live in Colorado, Georgia, Maryland, Massachusetts, New Jersey, or Vermont, you can obtain one for free—those states are required by law to provide, on request, one free copy of your credit report each year.

No matter where you live, you can obtain a free credit report if, within the previous sixty days, you've been denied credit, insurance, or employment based on your credit history. If you have reason to believe that your credit report contains inaccurate information, you may also be able to request a free copy.

The Loan Application and Approval Process

When you apply for a mortgage on a house (or for preapproval), the lender will want you to fill out a form that summarizes your financial situation. The lender will also want a copy of your credit report, a survey or official surveyor's drawing of the property, and an appraisal. The lender will handle the details and hire the necessary professionals, but you will pay the fees, which typically include the following:

• **Application fee.** Averages about $220. Charged to cover the lender's costs in reviewing your application and to make sure you're serious.

SMART SOURCES

Here's how to contact the three leading credit bureaus by phone and on the Web:

Equifax
800-997-2493
www.equifax.com

Experian
888-397-3742
www.experian.com

Trans Union
800-888-4213
www.tuc.com

SMART MONEY

If you've had credit problems, don't make things worse by falling for the scams of companies billing themselves as credit repair services. "The only way to truly 'fix' bad credit is to bring your payments up to date and keep them current," says Maxine Sweet, Vice President of Consumer Education at Experian. "So-called 'credit repair' clinics can do nothing for you that you can't do for yourself. Worse, many credit repair clinics have operated on the fringes—or even beyond the fringes—of the law."

• **Credit report.** Expect to pay about $48.

• **Appraisal fee.** Expect to pay about $290.

The good news is that most lenders (75 percent or so) charge an application fee that includes both the credit report and the appraisal. So your total cost to apply for a mortgage may be closer to $220, not $558 as you might expect if you were to add up these three ballpark figures. Other fees, like a "loan origination" fee amounting to 1 percent or more of the mortgage, are paid at the closing.

The Universal Residential Loan Application

You may meet at the loan officer's place of business, or the lender may send someone out to your home or office, but one way or another, you will have to supply *detailed* information about your financial life. After all, money is at stake. The information is usually collected on a form called the Universal Residential Loan Application (URLA).

The form—four legal-size pages—is approved by Fannie Mae, which is why it is so widely used. You can get a copy from your prospective lender, of course, but it's also readily available on the Internet, at Web sites like the Home Buyers Network (www.homebuyersnet.com/urla.htm). It can be found at many lender sites as well.

Mortgage Application Information You'll Need

Here is a list of the information and supporting documents most commonly needed in order to apply for a mortgage loan. You may need additional information or documents depending on the type of loan you're applying for, so be sure to check with the lender.

• Social Security numbers for all applicants.

• Address(es) for the past two years (including name and address of landlord, if applicable).

• Name, address, and income earned from all employers during the past twenty-four months.

• Copies of W-2 forms for the previous two years.

• Copy of most recent year-to-date pay stub.

• Name, address, account number, monthly payment, and current balance for all installment loans, revolving charge accounts, student loans, mortgage loans, and auto loans.

• Name, address, account number, and balance of all deposit accounts, including checking accounts, savings accounts, stocks, bonds, and others.

• Three most recent monthly statements for deposit accounts, stocks, bonds, and others.

F.Y.I.

According to Waterfield Mortgage Company in Ft. Wayne, Indiana, the time required to process a loan application used to be two weeks and the cost averaged $3,274. After installing new software, the firm cut the time to several days and the cost to $2,615. Lenders want to get all they can, but the mortgage application fee doesn't cover the actual cost of processing a loan.

SMART MONEY

If you're self-employed or simply can't face the prospect of assembling a mountain of paperwork, "low-doc" or "no-doc" loans may be the answer. With a low-doc loan, the lender asks for minimal paperwork ("documentation")—often no more than one pay stub and a credit report. With a no-doc, not even those items are required.

"The good thing about this kind of mortgage," says Norwest Mortgage Account Executive Dan Dawes, "is that it's not just for people who are self-employed. It's for anyone who walks and breathes and has good credit. And for people who are self-employed, it's ideal. They're writing off everything they can, leaving them with a net income that won't allow them to qualify for a more conventional loan."

• If you choose to include income from child support/alimony, copies of court records verifying payment history or copies of cancelled checks.

If you are applying for a Veteran's Administration Loan (explained in the next chapter):

• DD-214, Certificate of Eligibility, or statement from your commanding officer if you are on active duty.

If you are self-employed or paid by commission:

• Previous two years' federal income tax returns with all schedules and a year-to-date profit-and-loss statement.

If you own other property:

• Address and current market value of each property.

• Any debt owed on the property, along with lender's name, address, account number, monthly payment, and current balance.

• Previous two years' federal income tax returns with all schedules.

• If the property is rented, a copy of the lease.

If you have filed for bankruptcy in the last seven years:

• Copy of petition and discharge, handwritten explanation of reason for bankruptcy, and evidence of excellent credit since the bankruptcy.

Low-Doc and No-Doc Loans for the Self-Employed

Self-employed people and business owners don't fit the standard mortgage application mold. Unlike the vast majority of people, they don't get regular paychecks. And they make every effort to reduce their taxes by taking every legal deduction available. As a result, the net income shown on their tax forms may be too low for them to qualify for a given mortgage.

The solution for many who don't fit the mold is a *low-doc* (low-documentation) or *no-doc* (no-documentation) loan. With a low-doc loan, the lender may ask for nothing more than one recent pay stub and a bank statement. The lender may or may not pull your credit report. With a no-doc, the lender provides financing based on your stated employment, bank account, and asset information and conducts no verifications at all.

The catch is that you'll have to make a down payment of 20 to 25 percent (or more) and pay an interest rate of about one point above the market rate. Still, if you have assets and are self-employed, low-doc/no-doc may be the way to go.

The National Home Ownership Strategy

In November 1994, President Clinton launched a program called the National Home Ownership Strategy: Partners in the American Dream. The goal of the program is to generate up to 8 million additional homeowners by the year 2000, raising the nation's home ownership rate from 64 percent to a historically high level of 67.5 percent. Some sixty-five public and private housing organizations, led by the Department of Housing and Urban Development (HUD), are currently participating in the effort.

The idea of this initiative is to make home ownership much more affordable—particularly for low- and moderate-income individuals and families—by cutting closing and financing costs and easing down-payment requirements. The program is also designed to open housing markets by reducing regulatory and discriminatory barriers, and to increase awareness of home ownership opportunities by providing information and educational offerings.

A nationwide home ownership counseling program will soon be offered through the American Home Ownership Education and Counseling Institute. The Institute is expected to be fully operational by early 1999. In the meantime, call 800-569-4287 for the name of a home counseling agency in your area. Counselors are available to help you with every phase of finding housing, whether you want to rent or buy.

For more information, visit the National Home Ownership Strategy Web site (www.uha.org/ strategy/welcome.html). From here you can call up a list of national and local partners. You can then contact specific partners for more information on home-ownership and home-financing programs.

....

Finding the Right Mortgage

Where to Shop for a Mortgage

If you're qualified to "buy" a mortgage, there are lots and lots of people who would love to "sell" you one, and that's precisely how you should approach the mortgage-shopping process. You're the customer. The product is money. And if the lenders don't persuade you to buy, they don't make a profit. In other words, don't let yourself be intimidated by all the financial information you have to reveal or weakened by how much you want a particular house.

And don't give up. Many, many people, agencies, and institutions are quite interested in seeing you buy a house. After all, home ownership is not only good for you, it's good for the country, the economy, and your local community. As we'll see in a moment, many special programs are available, particularly for first-time buyers. But right now let's look at where you should go to shop for the best deal.

Start with a Mortgage Broker

One increasingly popular way to shop for a mortgage is to call a mortgage broker. In years past, mortgage brokers were used primarily by people who had such bad credit histories that they usually could not get financing any other way. No more. Today mortgage brokers have become professional mortgage finders and facilitators.

Mortgage brokers are like independent insurance agents. They typically work with several large mortgage companies to get you the best deal. Mortgage brokers thus serve as lender sales representatives and loan officers. They walk you through the application and handle all the paperwork. In return, the lender pays the broker a commission on your loan. Commissions range from about half a point to two points, but the cost is paid by the lender instead of coming out of your pocket. That's because without the mortgage broker, the lender would have to pay an employee to execute the same tasks. This way, the lender pays only when a loan is approved.

Before you contact a mortgage broker you will want to go over the latest offers and rates published in your local newspaper, which will give you a basis of comparison. A good mortgage broker will be quite familiar with these rates and with who's offering them. And he or she will also be aware of deals that are not advertised in the paper.

According to information published by the National Association of Mortgage Brokers (NAMB) in McLean, Virginia, the typical mortgage broker works with forty or more wholesale lenders at any one time. Indeed, if you want to make sure that the person or company you are contacting is really a mortgage broker, ask if they belong to NAMB, and find out which mortgage lenders they work with.

Mortgage Banks and Traditional Possibilities

Mortgage banks are the next place to check. These organizations specialize in mortgages and thus may be among the least expensive alternatives. They also tend to offer more options than

SMART SOURCES

For more information on mortgage brokers, contact NAMB. If you visit the association's Web site, select the "State Chapters" icon to find out how to contact your state's NAMB organization.

National Association of Mortgage Brokers (NAMB)
703-610-9009
www.namb.org

SMART SOURCES

Here's how to contact the top mortgage banks in the U.S.:

Norwest Mortgage
800-405-8067
www.norwest.com

Countrywide Home
  Loans
800-570-9888
www.countrywide.com

Chase Manhattan
  Mortgage
800-678-1051
www.chase.com

traditional banks and savings and loan associations (S&Ls). You should know, however, that mortgage banks are among the main lenders used by mortgage brokers, so if you can't get a better rate by dealing directly with a mortgage bank, you may find it less of a hassle to go with a mortgage broker who has a relationship with such a bank. As long as you're paying the same, let your local mortgage broker do all the work.

Your next best choice is likely to be your credit union, particularly if it is a large one. After that are your local savings and loans associations. S&Ls, in fact, were created specifically to promote thrift and home ownership. Commercial banks, many of which have mortgage-lending divisions, are probably the next logical choice.

It goes without saying that when evaluating loan deals, it is crucial to make sure that you are comparing apples to apples. Before making a selection, find out about all the fees, points, and special charges involved with each lender's offer. Remember that the total cost of a loan one lender will make to someone in your situation should not be dramatically less than that of another lender. If there is a huge apparent disparity between two offers, watch out! Once again, money is the "perfect product." So one way or another, a lender will always get the going rate.

The Mortgage APR Fallacy

The government requires mortgage lenders to quote an annual percentage rate (APR) in addition to the interest rate of the loan. Unfortunately, the rules for calculating APR have not been clearly defined.

S&Ls, Your "Local" Mortgage Lender

I didn't think our situation was unusual," says Tom, a service technician trainee with a copier and office equipment firm. "But I guess if you're going to have your mortgage cosigned by your parents, you don't meet the 'standard' guidelines.

"I called a few banks and was getting really discouraged when a buddy of mine suggested going with an S&L. He and his wife bought a duplex. They live in one part and rent out the other part to help with the payments. He told me mortgage brokers and bankers wouldn't touch the deal because it wasn't typical, but a savings and loan was willing to work with them.

"I contacted my friend's loan officer the next day. He set up a meeting at his office with me, my wife, and our parents, and we worked it out. The loan officer said we'd gotten a really good price on the property, and the schools are considered to be among the best in the state."

The loan officer also explained to Tom and his wife that, because many S&Ls are "portfolio lenders" who hold on to the loans they originate instead of selling them on the secondary market, they are not bound by Fannie Mae and similar underwriting ratios and requirements. And because they are local, they know the area and are well positioned to judge the risks associated with a given property.

Of course, they can't compete with the huge national firms on price. Typically rates will be an eighth to a quarter of a point higher at an S&L. But as one S&L loan officer says, "If a loan has a story, we're the lender to contact first."

Different lenders make different assumptions about how (or even if) the index used to peg the rate on an adjustable-rate mortgage (ARM) will change over time. And on a 30-year fixed-rate loan, the APR formula amortizes points over the full term of the loan, but most borrowers don't hold such loans to term. The only way to compare the APRs quoted by different lenders is to fully understand the assumptions each has made, a chore that is likely to be more trouble than it is worth.

Guaranteed-Loan Solutions to Home Financing

In the best of all possible worlds, you would be able to turn to one source for a complete list of all the mortgage deals of any sort available to you and make your selection. Unfortunately, while there are Internet Web sites that offer extensive options, no single master list of this sort is available. That's why many prospective home buyers find mortgage brokers so appealing.

Still, it is enormously helpful to be aware of the many nonconventional options that exist. You may have to do a little digging, but special deals and programs are available. Of particular interest are the programs made possible by some government or quasi-government agencies. The most popular and widely used programs include the following:

• **FHA loans.** Insured by the Department of Housing and Urban Development's (HUD) Federal Housing Administration. The required down payment is 3 to 5 percent of the FHA appraisal value or purchase price, whichever is lower. Maximum loan limit varies with the average cost of housing in a given area. FHA loans can be assumed by a buyer. And when rates drop, they can be "streamlined" to the lower rate with no points or other charges.

FHA does not require a flawless credit record, nor does it set maximum income limits. You can even add closing costs to the mortgage and borrow the entire amount. But FHA loans may cost a bit more due to the higher cost of government (versus private) mortgage insurance.

In addition to the standard FHA 203(b) loan, the agency offers FHA ARM (251) with adjustable rates, FHA GPM (Graduated Payment Mortgage), FHA/VA 203 (v) for veterans, and FHA 203(k) for those who want to incorporate into their mortgage a loan for rehabilitating a home.

• **VA loans.** These loans are available to those who have been honorably discharged from the armed services. Qualified veterans can buy a house costing up to $203,000 with no down payment. The interest rate offered is often lower than with other kinds of loans. Qualification guidelines are more flexible than those for either FHA or conventional loans.

VA loans can be assumed by nonveterans when the original borrower sells the house. Also, the VA often has an inventory of homes to sell due to repossessions. Such homes are available to vets and nonvets alike. Some states also have programs for veterans similar to those offered by the VA, so be sure to check.

• **HUD-insured loans and HUD houses.** FHA loans are only one of many kinds of HUD-backed mortgages. There are loans for rehabs, for those with special credit risks, for buying condominiums, for disaster victims, and for those wishing to make a property more energy-efficient after they buy. Down payments may be as low as 3 percent. For a complete overview, contact your nearest HUD office.

Also, like the VA, HUD often has an inventory of homes "taken back" from FHA borrowers who have defaulted. Depending on market conditions, you may be able to buy such a home with as little

SMART SOURCES

For more information
about the loans and
special home-buying
programs discussed in
this section, call or
visit the Web sites
listed here:

FHA Loans
202-708-2495
www.hud.gov/fha/
   fhainfo.html
(General information)

www.hud.gov/mortprog.
   html
(Click on "FHA Mortgage
   Limits" for current
   local loan maximums)

VA Loans
800-827-1000
www.va.gov/vas/loan/
   index.htm

HUD-Insured Loans
   and HUD Houses
202-708-1422
www.hud.gov/local.
   html
(Click on the name of
   your state to find the
   nearest HUD office)

as a few hundred dollars down. Contact HUD for a list of real estate agents authorized to sell such homes in your area.

• **RHS loans.** The Rural Housing Service, a branch of the U.S. Department of Agriculture, offers low-interest-rate loans with no down-payment requirements to low- and moderate-income people in rural areas or small towns.

• **Fannie Mae and Freddie Mac loans.** Fannie Mae and Freddie Mac are government-created private companies with different business strategies but with the same mission: Make more money available for lending by selling bundles of home mortgages on the secondary market.

Both companies create products for lenders to offer consumers—particularly first-time home buyers. In most cases, these products are limited to those whose income is no greater than 100 percent of the area median income. They are almost always a very good deal. Ask prospective lenders about any offerings related to Fannie Mae's Community Home Buyer's Program. That program's 3/2 option allows you to put 3 percent down and obtain 2 percent as a gift from family and friends or as a grant from an agency or organization.

Another program called Fannie 97 lets you borrow 97 percent of the purchase price, while making a 3 percent down payment and having your closing costs paid by gifts or grants and loans from nonprofits or government agencies. The Fannie Neighbors program adds still more flexibility for those purchasing a home within certain cities and areas. (Freddie Mac's Discover the Gold is similar to Fannie 97, and it offers loans with as little as 5 percent down.)

• **State and local housing finance agencies.** *Money* magazine columnist Beth Kobliner calls these agencies "one of the best-kept secrets of home buying." They don't advertise, but they often have bond-financed mortgage programs that offer money at one to four points lower than the going bank rate with down-payment requirements ranging from 5 percent to "nothing down."

You can get the names and numbers of your local housing finance agency (HFA) by contacting the National Council of State Housing Agencies (202-624-7710, www.ncsha.org). Since funds are limited and tend to go fast, you will want to make sure you know when the next round of bond money will be available and be prepared to act quickly.

Creative Financing Solutions

If you are coming to the conclusion that the number of ways to get yourself into a home are nearly infinite, you are very much on the right track. You now have some idea of the leading government programs and loan guarantees that are available. But you'll want to check for updates when the time comes, and you'll want to push even further by looking into any programs offered by the social, religious, community, or other organizations you may have joined. Remember, government and private programs typically don't have money to spend on advertising, so it's up to you to actively research the possibilities.

Even if, despite your best efforts, no help seems to be available, don't give up. For beyond

SMART SOURCES

RHS Loans
202-720-4323
www.rurdev.usda.gov

Fannie Mae Loans
800-832-2345
www.fanniemae.com

Freddie Mac Loans
800-373-3343
www.freddiemac.com

State and Local Housing Finance Agencies (HFAs)
National Council of State Housing Agencies
202-624-7710
www.ncsha.org
(Click on "State HFA Directory" to find your local housing finance agency)

the traditional, beyond the loan guarantees, there are still more options and possibilities, including the following:

• **Builder financing.** If you're buying a house in a new development, be sure to see what kind of financing the builder may be able to offer. Lenders are often happy to give builders special rates for originating loans, since many do so in such volumes. As long as the rates and terms the builder offers you are at least as good as those available on the market, this may be a good option.

• **Seller financing.** Sometimes called "seller take-back." You give the seller 5 to 10 percent of the agreed price in cash as your down payment and sign a note agreeing to make regular monthly payments at a given interest rate. Buyers like it because there are no points or other lending fees. Sellers like it because of the monthly income stream it generates and because the loan is secured by a property they know well. Should the buyer default, the seller can foreclose. And should the seller decide to cash in, there are any number of mortgage companies that can buy the note.

The main caveat with seller financing is to make sure you have your agreement drawn up or reviewed by a qualified attorney. (In some parts of the country these arrangements are called "land sales contracts.")

• **Family financing.** If your family has the money, they can invest it by loaning it to you to purchase a home. Make sure everything is covered with the proper legal documents. And if you plan to deduct the interest on the loan for tax purposes, make sure that the rate you are paying your family is close to the going commercial rate. Otherwise the IRS may want you to treat any interest savings as a gift. Above all, get advice from a competent CPA or attorney who can make sure you cross all the legal T's and dot all the I's.

• **Buy-down mortgages.** With this approach, the seller or your family or someone else helps you out with the mortgage for its first few years by paying the difference between the current interest rate and the rate you are paying. Suppose you can't qualify for a current rate of 8 percent. Your buy-down partner agrees to pay on a 3-2-1 arrangement—3 percent the first year, 2 percent the second, and 1 percent the third. After that, you're on your own.

Assuming a steady rate of 8 percent, this would mean that you'd pay 5 percent the first year, 6 percent the second, and 7 percent in the third year. In the fourth year, after all your raises and promotions, you would presumably be in a good position to take on the full 8 percent.

For a loan of $100,000 and a prevailing rate of 8 percent, this little exercise would cost your buy-down partner about $5,000 over three years, while making it possible for you to buy the home right now. (Because buy-downs are more complex than standard mortgages, look for a portfolio lender who does not plan to sell your mortgage on the secondary market.)

• **Lease with an option to buy.** If you can afford the monthly payments but have no way of coming up with the down payment, this option may be the right one for you. First, you negotiate the sale price of the home with the seller. Then you buy a one-year option by paying the seller a nonrefundable option fee. You move in and start paying rent.

F.Y.I.

Some lenders will make a loan equal to 125 to 150 percent of a property's value. The idea is to provide the borrower with enough money to buy a house and to fix, repair, and refurbish it—without cashing in retirement plans or selling stock or property. Lenders view this as a combination mortgage and personal loan secured by both the house and by the borrower's other assets. Rates are typically two points above the bank prime. Be sure to consult a tax accountant regarding the interest that can be deducted on this type of loan.

The seller credits a portion of your monthly rent toward your down payment. Everything is negotiable, but rent credits of 34 to 50 percent are not uncommon. When you reach the necessary down-payment amount, you can exercise your option to buy the house at the previously agreed upon price.

This is a relatively complicated arrangement, so make sure that you have it handled by a qualified attorney—one with lots of experience drawing up lease/option agreements for residential purchases.

• **Shared-appreciation mortgages.** Here the lender loans you money at a below-market rate in exchange for a percentage of any profit you make when you sell the property. This type of mortgage is often sponsored by nonprofit associations using Community Development Block Grant money to help low- and moderate-income families buy a home.

• **Real estate owned (REO) and sheriff's sales.** The last thing a lender wants to do is to foreclose on a house, but sometimes it becomes necessary. Details vary with the lender, but most are quite eager to have someone take the property off their hands and are thus willing to give you a good deal. Similar low-cost opportunities exist whenever a locality is forced to sell a house because the owner failed to pay the property taxes.

Be Smart about Private Mortgage Insurance

In mortgage-speak, the loan-to-value (LTV) ratio of a property is the ratio of the loan amount to the value of the property. So if you put 20 percent down, the LTV is 80 percent (or "80 LTV"). If you put 5 percent down, the LTV is 95 percent, and so on.

Regardless of the kind of loan you get, if the LTV is greater than 80 percent—which means you have put less than 20 percent down—you will probably have to buy private mortgage insurance (PMI). The lender is the beneficiary of such a policy, but you pay the premiums.

The premium can range anywhere from 0.22 percent to 0.9 percent of the loan amount. As with every other kind of insurance, the rate is based on the underwriter's assessment of risk. And private mortgage insurance companies tend to look for the same things lenders do when it comes to income, years of employment, credit history, and assets.

Fortunately, many lenders will let you drop PMI once your down payment and principal payments bring your equity to 20 percent. But be sure to ask. The onus is on you to monitor the situation and to take action when you get to 20 percent equity, although legislation has recently been introduced in Congress to force lenders to accept this responsibility themselves.

To take things a step further, however, it is worth considering the opportunity costs involved.

If you have or can raise enough money to make a 20 percent down payment, should you do so? You will need to run the numbers yourself, but you might be better off making a 10 percent down payment, paying the PMI premiums, and investing the remaining 10 percent.

Assume, for example, that the house you want to buy costs $120,000 and that you do indeed have the $24,000 necessary to make a 20 percent down payment. According to the PMI company Triad Guaranty Insurance Corporation (www.tgic.com), the average premium on a 90 LTV loan is 0.52 percent. So, if you make a 10 percent down payment ($12,000), the loan amount will be $108,000, and you will owe about $562 a year for PMI. But, more important, you will be able to invest the remaining $12,000.

Leaving aside any tax considerations, if you can invest that money at 10 percent, you'll earn $1,200 a year, enough to pay your PMI premium and still have a profit of over $600. And if you put it into a 401(k) plan that involves some kind of matching from your employer, not only will it grow immediately, it will grow and compound tax-free until you retire.

Watch Out for Prepayment Penalties

Whenever possible, you will want to avoid any mortgage that includes a prepayment penalty. This usually amounts to 1 to 2 percent of the mortgage should you pay it off at any time within the first two to five years. There are at least two common situations when such penalties can possibly affect you.

The first is when you want to move to a different house. Unless the mortgage can be assumed by your buyer, that buyer will pay you money that you will then use to pay off your mortgage. The second situation occurs when you want to refinance. That means paying off your current mortgage and replacing it with a mortgage offering a lower interest rate.

In years past, people applied the "2-2-2 Rule" to determine when refinancing was likely to be worthwhile. The idea was that if you've been in your home for two years, intend to stay at least two more years, and the refinanced rate is at least two points lower than your current rate, refinancing made good sense.

Today some experts suggest that a drop in rates of even one half of 1 percent can make refinancing worthwhile—if the attendant costs are wrapped into the loan or paid by the mortgage broker. Such loans are called "zero-cost" refinancings because, in exchange for about three-eighths of a point in the rate, all other fees are paid.

It is true that "your mileage may vary," but clearly, whether you think you'll be moving or refinancing in the next few years, it just makes good sense to avoid a mortgage with a prepayment penalty.

SMART SOURCES

Here are some of the leading mortgage- and interest-related Internet sites you might want to explore:

The Motley Fool/E-loan
www.eloan.com
www.fool.com
(On AOL, use the
    keyword FOOL)

HSH Associates
www.hsh.com

HomeShark
www.homeshark.com

Fannie Mae HomePath
www.homepath.com
(Click on "Site Map"
    and then on "Search
    for a Lender")

Mortgage Market Information Services, Inc.
www.interest.com

First Manhattan
    Funding, Inc.
fmfinc.com
(A California company
    with associate
    lenders nationwide)

Should You Pay Off Your Mortgage Faster?

There is usually nothing in a loan agreement to prevent you from paying off your mortgage faster by simply increasing the amount of your monthly payment. You can specify that you want the excess applied to the principal, thus reducing the amount you owe and shortening the term of the loan. According to Jeffrey Tuchman, a mortgage consultant in Pleasantville, New York, "As a general rule, on a 30-year mortgage, you save $3 for every $1 you prepay. On an after-tax basis, you get back $2 for every $1 you prepay."

Another way to accelerate things is to make arrangements to pay your mortgage biweekly. With a biweekly mortgage, you make twenty-six payments a year (one every other week) instead of twelve monthly payments. This is equivalent to making a thirteenth monthly payment each year, and it enables you to pay off a 30-year mortgage in fewer than twenty-two years, for a savings of thousands—even tens of thousands—of dollars.

Not all lenders offer biweeklies, and those that do may insist on deducting the payment automatically from your checking account. Some may even charge you for converting to a biweekly arrangement. Before buying such a conversion, check to see if the lender will let you prepay for free by adding any additional amount you wish to your regular monthly payment.

Keep in mind, though, that as much as you might love the idea of owning your home free and clear, prepaying your mortgage may not be a good financial strategy. Before committing yourself to any prepayment approach, consider the opportunity cost of investing that extra money elsewhere.

According to Lynn Brenner, author of *Smart Questions to Ask Your Financial Advisers,* "If your mortgage costs eight percent a year, that's what you'll earn on your prepayment. Compare that return with what you'd earn in other comparably safe investments, like a CD or paying off credit cards. If you pay eighteen percent on credits cards, don't even think about prepaying an eight percent mortgage instead!"

Coming Up with the Down Payment: Time to Get Creative

If you're a first-time home buyer, no one needs to tell you what an enormous hurdle it's likely to be to scrape together the money needed to make a down payment. By now you are well aware that lenders like to see you put 20 percent down but that programs exist that can make it possible for you to put down as little as 3 percent. Yet even 3 percent can amount to thousands of dollars. And, as has been emphasized repeatedly, the down payment is only the largest star in an entire galaxy of costs associated with buying a home.

What to do? Traditionally, young people have relied on their parents to offer substantial financial help when making a down payment. The only catch is that lenders tend to view help of this sort

SMART DEFINITION

Bi-weekly mortgage payments

The majority of mortgages call for monthly payments, which is to say, every four weeks. But you can dramatically cut both the term of the loan and the amount of interest you pay by paying half the monthly mortgage amount every two weeks. For example, assuming a 30-year, $100,000 loan at a fixed rate of 8 percent, making bi-weekly payments will reduce the term of the loan to 22.9 years and save you about $225 a month, or $45,665.23 in interest payments over the course of the loan. Ask your lender for details. And note that even with a monthly mortgage, you can always pay more than the amount due and ask that the extra be devoted to paying off the principal.

as a loan that increases your indebtedness. You and your spouse and your combined sets of parents may agree that the money is a gift, but the lender may see it as an obligation that you and your significant other must pay, just as you must pay your MasterCard and Visa bills.

That's why it can be crucial to raise this matter early on with your lender of choice. The lender will want to see the entire paper trail showing where the money is coming from, in any case, but you should show the lender that you have thought things through and be prepared to lay out the details right from the start. The lender may then ask you to supply a "gift letter." This is a form stating that a relative is giving you the money to help you buy a home and that you will not be asked to pay it back.

Tapping Savings and Investment Accounts

Traditionally, people save and invest until they have enough money to start looking for a house. Then they liquidate their investments to make a down payment. If you have a choice, however, you might want to consider other options, since this may not be the smartest way to handle things. For example, if you have $5,000 in a mutual fund that earns an average of 12 percent a year, you might be better off holding on to the fund and making a smaller down payment. You'll pay a slightly higher interest rate and have to buy private mortgage insurance. But your interest will be tax deductible, and even with the PMI premium, you probably won't be paying 12 percent.

Certainly you will need *some* cash. Just don't automatically assume that you must sell all your investments. You may even be able to pledge your securities in lieu of making a cash down payment.

Merrill Lynch's "Mortgage 100" program, for example, offers financing for up to 100 percent of a first or second home or investment property. You place the required securities in a pledge account but are able to continue trading and collecting dividends as long as the value of the securities does not drop below some predefined point. Another Merrill Lynch program, called Parent Power, uses a similar approach to make it possible for parents or sponsors to help a family member finance a home while preserving their own investment strategies.

For more information on these programs, contact Merrill Lynch (800-854-7154, www.plan. ml.com). And while they may be the best known, you'll find that mortgage banks and similar institutions have "pledge" offerings of their own.

Borrowing from Retirement Accounts

One of the wonders of modern times is the miracle of tax-deferred compound interest. If at age thirty-five you were to put $5,000 into a tax-deferred retirement account earning 10 percent a year—and leave it there—by the time you turned sixty-five, it would have grown to more than $87,000. If the account is a 401(k) or similar account in which your contributions were in some way matched by your employer, the sum would be larger still.

The key, of course, is the compounding. Each

F.Y.I.

For mathematical reasons that need not concern us, the Rule of 72 will tell you how soon your money will double at a given rate of interest. All you have to do is divide 72 by the interest rate your investment is earning. Thus, if your money is earning 10 percent, it will double in 7.2 years. If it is earning 15 percent, it will double in 4.8 years. This is why even a small amount invested in a tax-deferred retirement account at an early age can grow into such a nest egg by the time you retire.

year you earn interest not only on your contribution but also on the interest it has earned. But it takes time to work. Borrowing from a retirement account interferes with this engine. Add to this the fact that you're dealing with the money you plan to live on after you retire, and you may want to think twice about raiding this particular piggy bank.

Your options will depend on the details of your employer's plan. Some plans do not permit loans for any purpose. Others limit you to borrowing for a home or for college. Typically, you'll pay only 1 to 3 percent over the prime rate banks charge their best customers, but at least you'll be paying it to yourself, since both principal and interest go right back into your account.

Unfortunately, though, you will be paying yourself back with after-tax dollars instead of the pre-tax dollars with which you funded the account. And the money you repay will be taxed again when you withdraw it after you retire. The interest may or may not be tax-deductible, so check with your accountant before pursuing this option.

The maximum you can borrow without penalty is $50,000, or 50 percent of the assets in your account, whichever is less. Anything over that will be treated as a taxable withdrawal on which you will owe a 10 percent penalty if you are younger than fifty-nine and a half. The typical term of such loans is five years, although terms may be as long as thirty years if the money is used to buy a principal residence. Should you quit or be fired, you will probably have to repay the entire loan immediately or face taxes and a penalty on the outstanding balance.

Roth IRA Options

A new form of Individual Retirement Account (IRA) became available on January 1, 1998. Known as a Roth IRA, it is funded with after-tax dollars. But, as with all IRAs, your earnings grow tax-free. You can withdraw your contributions at any time, but what really sets the Roth IRA apart is that you can withdraw your profits as well, tax-free, after five years under certain conditions. One of those conditions is that you want to buy or build a first house for yourself, your spouse, your child, grandchild, or parents.

The maximum amount of earnings you can withdraw for this purpose is $10,000. That is a lifetime limit, though you do not have to take it out all at once. And it's important to note that a "first-time home buyer" is defined as someone who has not owned a home during the past two years. If you're married, your spouse cannot have owned a home during that period either.

Borrowing from Your Life Insurance

Experts agree that term life insurance makes the most financial sense for the majority of people. That's because it is pure insurance, not insurance combined with an investment component, as is the case with whole-life or universal-life policies. Still, millions of people own policies of this sort that have accumulated substantial cash value over the years. And, as the life insurance salesperson is sure to have emphasized, you can borrow against that cash value—which is to say, the cash value can be used as collateral for a loan.

There are at least two things to keep in mind before borrowing against a policy's cash value. First, the death benefit will be reduced by the loan amount. Second, the effective interest rate will be about what you'd pay on a home-equity loan or on a loan secured by stocks or mutual fund shares, not the stated policy loan rate.

That's because while insurance companies typically pay an interest rate on your cash value about equal to that of a U.S. Treasury bond, most reduce the percentage they pay on the cash value you have borrowed against. For example, a stated loan rate of 6 percent may sound great, but if the company reduces the rate it normally pays on the cash value you are borrowing against by 2 percent, your actual interest rate is not 6 percent, it's 8 percent.

CHAPTER 10

....

The Closing

THE KEYS

• Closing on a home is not the time for negotiation.

• Your sales contract should include a provision allowing you a final "walk-through" inspection of the property just prior to the closing itself.

• Your lender is required to provide you with a good-faith list of your closing expenses within three business days of accepting your application. But you can negotiate some of those expenses.

• Be sure to get "owner's title insurance" in addition to the lender-required lender title insurance.

• Do your best to hold out for splitting any transfer taxes with the seller.

• Take an active role in the closing—don't just let it happen.

The Closing. It sounds like the title of a Stephen King novel. Ominous, scary, and final. Also, "expensive." No matter how well you prepare, no matter how well you understand what you will have to pay, the experience of writing out check after check will always remain breathtaking, to say the least. Some people find it difficult to believe that the whole thing isn't one big shakedown.

Well, it isn't, of course. Not that governments, attorneys, lenders, real estate agents, and others necessarily resist the temptation to take advantage of someone in the midst of a major life event, particularly one that involves a lot of money. But this is nothing new. You won't be here to protest, but it would just kill you to see what governments, courts, attorneys, and other professionals take from your estate after your final major life event.

There may not be much you can do about it in either case, but you owe it to yourself to be informed. And, after all, the closing is both the end of your house-hunting process and the beginning of your life in your new home. After you've read this chapter, it won't be scary at all.

Closing, Settlement, and Escrow

As with nearly everything else about real estate, the procedures followed for finalizing a home-sale deal are largely governed by local custom. In California and many western states, for example, it is common to use an *escrow agent*. The escrow agent—usually a lawyer, an escrow firm, or a title company—serves as a third party who holds the money, prepares the documents, and mediates any disputes. In most other regions of the country, the *closing*, or the *settlement* as it may be called, takes place at a meeting attended by the buyers, the sellers, their attorneys, an agent from the bank, someone from the title insurance company, and one or more real estate agents.

However it is conducted, the closing is the point at which all the details are finalized and all the agreements are executed. It is characterized by the writing of many checks and the signing of many documents. It ends when the seller or escrow agent hands you the keys.

The one thing the closing is not supposed to be is a negotiating session. By the time you reach the closing, all issues regarding who will pay for what, the personal property that will be left in the home, when the sellers will leave, and any other part of the deal should have been agreed to. The closing simply puts everything into effect.

Four Types of Closing Costs

You know going in that at the very least the closing will involve you handing a certified check for the outstanding balance of the purchase price to the seller. If you take it a bit further, it is only fair that you pay the seller for any heating oil left in the home's tanks (should you live in a region that heats with oil) and a pro-rated portion of the real estate taxes the seller has paid. Certainly someone has to pay the fees of the home inspector and termite/pest control person, and probably it should be you since then there will be no doubt about who these professionals are working for.

SMART SOURCES

For excellent information on closing costs, get the booklet "Buying Your Home: Settlement Costs and Helpful Information" [HUD-398-H(4)]. Among many other things, the booklet contains the "HUD-1 Settlement Statement" that is widely used in the real estate industry. The file is available in MS Word and PDF/Acrobat formats at: www.hud.gov/fha/res/sfhrestc.html. Or go to www.hud.gov and select "HUD on Your Side: Consumer Information" from the main menu, then click on "Buying a Home." (Also, check out www.pueblo.gsa.gov/housing.htm for even more house-related information.)

If you're not online, order publication 112E from the Government Printing Office Consumer Information Center in Pueblo, Colorado. The cost is $1.75. Call 719-948-4000.

What's likely to throw you, if you are not prepared, are all the other very unfamiliar fees, many of which can amount to several hundred or several thousand dollars. That's why you need to know that there are four main categories of closing costs:

• Charges for establishing and transferring ownership.

• Taxes and fees paid to state and local governments.

• Costs associated with your mortgage loan financing.

• Seller-reimbursement and miscellaneous costs.

Ownership Transfer Charges

To most people, the closing costs associated with establishing and transferring ownership are probably the least familiar. They can include:

• Settlement or closing fee.

• Notary and attorney fees.

• Document preparation.

• Abstract or title search.

• Title examination.

• Title insurance binder.

- Lender's title insurance premium.

- Owner's title insurance premium.

The settlement or closing fee is paid to the settlement agent, escrow holder, or other individual responsible for overseeing the closing. In some states, the title company conducts the closing. In other states, buyer and seller each hire an attorney to do it. In many western states, an escrow agent is used. If a fee is charged for conducting a closing, it should be split between the buyer and seller since both parties benefit from the person's services.

Documents like the deed to a property must be signed by the "grantors" (the owners). The notary fee is charged for the cost of having someone who is licensed as a notary public swear to the fact that those people named in such documents really did sign them. As for the attorney's fees, you may be required by your lender to pay for an attorney to examine the title binder. The title binder is a document giving immediate insurance coverage in cases where the full policy cannot be issued by the closing date.

Some title companies charge a fee to cover the costs of preparing the deed of trust and other final legal papers.

Title-Related Charges

The title-related charges on the list above are probably the least understood of all, but here's an example that will help make things clear. Suppose that a year after you buy your home, John Smith comes forward and claims that he inherited the property from his grandfather, and that Bob and

SMART MONEY

In the real estate business the term "junk fees" refers to charges made by a lender to cover dubious expenses and so boost total profit. Perhaps the most notorious are "processing fees" or "document preparation fees." They are akin to fees for "dealer prep" when buying a car.

Newsweek and *Washington Post* financial columnist Jane Bryant Quinn says, "Negotiate everything on the settlement sheet. Lenders have no business charging fees for 'processing' or 'document preparation.' That's what your loan-origination fee is supposed to cover." Many other lender-related closing-cost fees are negotiable, but the time to settle things is before you complete your mortgage application.

SMART DEFINITION

Cloud on title

According to John W. Reilly's *The Language of Real Estate*, this is "any document, claim, unreleased lien, or encumbrance which may impair or injure the title to a property or make the title doubtful because of its apparent or possible validity." Examples include a deed that one of several heirs failed to sign, a mortgage that has been paid and recorded but lacks a "satisfaction of mortgage" document, or an officially recorded option to buy the property granted to someone by a previous owner. Action by a court may be needed to clear the title in such cases. IRS, property-tax, and mechanic's liens must be satisfied (paid) by the current owner before the property can be sold.

Betty Jones did not have the right to sell it to you because they didn't actually own it.

Maybe the former owners never paid the contractor who put in the swimming pool and deck, so he filed a mechanic's lien against the property that no one discovered. The former owners are nowhere to be found, but the contractor is now on your doorstep, and he wants his money.

To protect itself against such possibilities, your lender will require you to pay for title insurance. Unlike conventional insurance, which is intended to protect you against loss from some *future* event, title insurance protects the policyholder against something that has *already happened,* like a forged deed somewhere in the past.

The title-related fees cover two main things. First, the title company will search the public records and prepare a title abstract. This is a full summary of all grants, conveyances, wills, records, and judicial proceedings affecting the title to a particular property. It will also include a statement of all liens and encumbrances affecting the property and their present status. The abstract will list ownership transfers in chronological order.

Once it is satisfied that the title has no "defects," the title insurance company will issue either a title insurance binder or the policy itself. The policy will promise to make good any losses suffered as a result of defects in the title. Typically, the policy will name the lender as the insured and the amount that will be insured will be the amount of the loan.

But what about insuring the amount of your down payment and increased equity? Unless you have "owner's title insurance," you could be in trouble if someone attacks your title. A court case will be required to settle the matter. That means lawyer's fees. Should you and your lender lose the case, the lender's costs and loan amount will be covered by the insurance. But your legal costs, down payment, and built-up equity will not be covered—unless you have your own title insurance coverage.

Government-Related Closing Costs

Closing costs paid in the form of taxes to state and local governments will be among the largest in total dollar amounts. First, there may be a fee for doing the paperwork needed to officially record your deed. In fact, the entire Recorder of Deeds office may be supported by such fees.

Second, there may possibly be transfer taxes— the equivalent of a sales tax on the home you're buying. Cities, counties, states, and any other governmental body that can manage it may try to get into the act. Why? Because they can. And because the "magic money" phenomenon discussed in chapter 7 dulls any pain you might feel and later express at the ballot box.

Taxes like this exist because they raise a significant amount of money and because they hit you at a time of emotional vulnerability. You just want to get the process finished, over with, so you can take possession of your new dwelling. A few hundred or a few thousand here and there in a $200,000 purchase—what does it matter? Let's just get it done. If you don't think that the people who instituted such taxes were aware of this, then you just might be interested in certain plots of prime bottom land now for sale in Florida, or maybe that bridge in Brooklyn.

SMART MONEY

According to Dr. Gary W. Eldred, executive director of the National Initiative for Home Ownership, adding your name to a lender's title insurance policy usually doesn't cost a great deal and "dramatically reduces the possibility that you'll be drawn into a long, drawn-out legal battle when some ex-husband of a long-ago owner shows up and claims that his ex-wife forged his name on the deed.

"If your sellers have title coverage, see if the policy can be updated and transferred to you. By sticking with the same company, you might save several hundred dollars. Or consider shopping around for the lowest premium. Finally, make sure you get an 'inflation endorsement' that will automatically boost your coverage as the value of your home increases."

There are only two things you can do about government-related taxes and fees. First, you can negotiate to have the seller pay part of them as you are working out your deal, long before closing. If you are unable to put together enough money to pay the sale price and the closing costs, the seller may be willing to help you with closing costs like these. From the seller's standpoint, it is all "magic money" too.

Second, once you take possession of the dwelling, you may be able to have your real estate taxes reduced by contesting your property's assessment. That's a complicated, legal subject beyond the scope of this book, but it is definitely something that you should consider looking into after you move in.

Lender-Related Costs

You will almost certainly have paid several mortgage- and lender-related costs before the closing. These include the application fee and fees for your credit report and property appraisal. At the closing, you may encounter fees for loan origination, "discount points," lender's inspection, a mortgage insurance application fee, and a fee that may be imposed if you assume the seller's mortgage.

Lenders may also require you to pay:

• Interest that accrues from the date of settlement to the first monthly payment.

• First year's private mortgage insurance (PMI) premium if you are putting less than 20 percent down. See chapter 9.

• Home-owner's insurance premium for the first year. You'll need to bring a paid-up policy to the closing. You might save money if you use the same firm for both home-owner's and auto insurance.

• Flood insurance premium for the first year. If the property has been flooded in the last one hundred to five hundred years, the lender will require this insurance.

• Property survey. This protects both you and the lender. If the lender does not require one, consider having one done yourself.

• Termite and other pest inspections.

• Lead-based paint inspections. Lead-based paint was outlawed in 1978. Children eating paint chips from houses built prior to that year may be in danger of lead poisoning. Buyers with young children may want to have such homes professionally inspected to determine the extent of the hazard and the cost of cleaning it up. For more information, contact the National EPA Lead-Based Paint Program at 919-558-0335, or visit the EPA Web site (www.epa.gov/opptintr/lead).

You may also have to deposit money with the lender for two months' worth of home-owner's and PMI premiums and city and county real estate taxes. Real estate and school taxes may be part of your total mortgage payment, in which case the lender escrows the money and then pays it to the authorities at the appropriate time, or you may be required to make such payments as lump sums by a certain day of the year.

F.Y.I.

Though sold by private companies, flood insurance is subsidized by the National Flood Insurance Program (NFIP), which is part of the Federal Emergency Management Agency (FEMA). For the name of a company offering flood insurance, call the NFIP toll-free response center (888-225-5356 ext. 445). The average flood insurance premium is $308 a year for $85,000 worth of coverage. You should insure your home for 100 percent of its replacement cost and buy enough additional insurance to cover the contents of your home. Either that, or move to higher ground.

Seller-Reimbursement Costs

Finally, there are settlement costs associated with evening out everything regarding the transition. The key word here is "pro-rated." For example, if the seller has paid a full year's real estate taxes but will end up living in the home for only half a year, you will reimburse the seller for the six months you will be living there.

Other adjustments include heating oil remaining in the tanks, home owner association fees or special assessments, and utility bills. You may want to ask gas, water, and electric companies for a special meter reading on the day of settlement and have the resulting bill mailed to the seller at his or her new address or to the settlement agent.

Conclusion: Welcome to Your New Home!

Buying a home is a "life event." So you owe it to yourself to take the entire day off from work. Schedule the closing in the morning if you can, and then spend the afternoon having a picnic lunch in your empty new home with your partner and maybe even your kids. You deserve it. No matter how many times you buy and sell a house, every transaction is different, and all of them are stressful. You deserve a celebration.

Your coauthors know a couple who unlocked the door to the two-hundred-year-old house they had just closed on and said, "House, we're here to take care of you." A split second later, the furnace came on. Perhaps opening the door let in cold air, but it was the month of May and all was warm. Maybe the vibrations created by uttering that statement affected the thermostat. But the thermostat was yards away. To this day, that couple believes that the house was responding in the only way it could, and that it was welcoming them. May the same happen to you!

THE BOTTOM LINE

Buying a new home is quite an experience. But if you've followed the advice in this book and taken care not to overpay, it is always worth it. Always. Come what may, you now own a piece of property. And property appreciates over time. Even if you decide to sell it in a few years, you're virtually certain to come out ahead or to at least break even.

So forget about "buyer's remorse." Relax and enjoy. There is no perfect home. But whether it's a detached house, a town house, a condominium apartment, or a big-city co-op, be it ever so humble, there really is no place like home!

Index

Books in the
Smart Guide™ Series

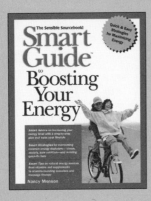

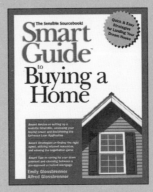

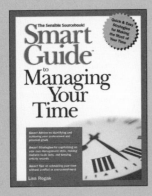